Ernest Hemingway's
THE SUN ALSO RISES

A CRITICAL COMMENTARY

LAWRENCE KLIBBE
PROFESSOR OF ROMANCE LANGUAGES
NEW YORK UNIVERSITY

MONARCH PRESS

NOTE:
THIS GUIDE IS INTENDED TO SUPPLEMENT AND ENHANCE,
AND IS NOT A SUBSTITUTE FOR, THE ORIGINAL WORK OF ART.

Published by
MONARCH PRESS
a Simon & Schuster division of
Gulf & Western Corporation
Simon & Schuster Building
1230 Avenue of the Americas
New York, N.Y. 10020

Standard Book Number: 0-671-00674-6

Library of Congress Catalog Card Number: 66-1766

Printed in the United States of America

CONTENTS

INTRODUCTION

Ernest Hemingway first gained widespread critical acclaim through the publication of *The Sun Also Rises* in 1926. However, the novel did not gain immediate popularity among the reading public until later years; in short, it did not hit the "best seller" list as did *A Farewell To Arms* in 1929. Prior to 1926, Hemingway was already regarded as a promising young writer of short stories, but his first novel, *The Torrents Of Spring,* published the same year as *The Sun Also Rises* and by the same publisher, Charles Scribner's Sons, was not a success. In *The Sun Also Rises,* Hemingway portrayed the problems and dilemmas of his age and his generation, the "lost generation" of the post-World War I period.

EARLY LIFE: Hemingway was born on July 21, 1899 in Oak Park, Illinois, a small, middle-class suburb of Chicago. Nothing in his early background indicated the bold writing he was to employ in his novels. The second of six children, Hemingway led a normal, active life of a schoolboy: although not especially popular, he took part in sports, debates, the school orchestra, wrote for and edited the school newspaper. Summers were spent outdoors in northern Michigan at a family camp. However, tensions evidently existed between the parents. Dr. Clarence E. Hemingway, a physician and enthusiastic outdoorsman, instilled in the young Ernest a love for hunting, fishing, and the natural life which he never abandoned. Grace Hall Hemingway, very pious and very active in church affairs, tried to interest the son in music and cultural pursuits; for example, Ernest had to play the cello. Although he ran away from home twice, and worked at a number of odd jobs, the young Hemingway saw his chance at escape from family and small-town pressures only when the

United States entered World War I in 1917. He immediately volunteered but was rejected because of an eye injury; nevertheless, he was accepted as an ambulance driver on the Italian front in early 1918.

WORLD WAR I: Hemingway's experiences in World War I fashioned much of his personal and literary outlook for the rest of his life. After leaving his job as a reporter on the *Kansas City Star* to join the ambulance corps in Italy, he was abruptly and brutally introduced to the facts of war. He witnessed a munitions explosion in Milan upon his arrival, and on July 8, 1918, just before his nineteenth birthday, he was severely wounded. He underwent twelve operations for removal of two hundred or so fragments of mortar shell but returned to the war as an infantry officer with the Italian Army. Two medals were awarded Hemingway by the Italian Government for his bravery during World War I. These experiences are vividly reflected in *A Farewell To Arms* in his hero, Frederic Henry, the depiction of war at close hand, and the whole attitude of Hemingway toward war and men at war. In *The Sun Also Rises,* Jake Barnes, the hero, also resembles somewhat Hemingway in his military service.

THE TWENTIES: Hemingway's restlessness in the period between the end of World War I and the publication of *A Farewell To Arms* becomes apparent in his many and varied activities during these ten years. His portrait of the expatriates in Paris and Spain in *The Sun Also Rises* is based on his own manifold contacts during the twenties. He married Hadley Richardson in 1921 but they were divorced in 1927 although he dedicated *The Sun Also Rises* to her in the previous year; and in 1927 he married Pauline Pfeiffer. Hemingway worked for the Toronto *Star* and *Star Weekly* from 1920 until 1924. In 1921 he returned to Europe and traveled widely throughout the continent; for example, he fell in love with Spain, which figures so prominently in his writings, during the twenties. His penchant for action was stimulated by his covering of the Greco-Turkish War, and the Greek retreat from Smyrna may be an antecedent for the Italian debacle of Caporetto, portrayed in *A Farewell To Arms*. Hemingway also covered the international events of this decade and met world statesmen, such as Lloyd George, Clemenceau, and Mussolini. Hemingway early grasped the dangers of Fascism and wrote scathingly of the Italian dictator whom he disliked immediately. In 1924 he settled in Paris to devote himself to his own writing and was introduced through Sherwood Anderson to the influential circle of Gertrude Stein. Her influence is noticeable in *The Sun Also Rises* at the very beginning when Hemingway quotes her as a motive for the book "You are all a lost generation."

Meanwhile, his stories had started to appear in magazines such as *Atlantic Monthly*. He published *Three Stories And Ten Poems* in 1923; *In Our Time*, a compendium of stories and vignettes, in 1924; the expanded version of these Nick Adams stories, *In Our Time*, in the United States in 1925; *The Torrents Of Spring*, a satirical, unsuccessful novel in the same year as *The Sun Also Rises*, 1926; and *A Farewell To Arms* in 1929. His father's suicide in 1928 affected him greatly.

THE THIRTIES: Hemingway's reputation mounted during these years; and as he entered the public limelight, the problem of distinguishing between the artist, the legend, and the man began to emerge. He traveled a great deal and used his trips to good advantage in the writings. He published thirty-one articles and stories in *Esquire; Death In The Afternoon* in 1932 and *Winner Take Nothing* in 1933; and *The Green Hills Of Africa* in 1935. When the Spanish Civil War broke out in 1936, Hemingway went to Spain as a correspondent for the North American Newspaper Alliance; his sympathies were on the side of the Loyalists against the forces of Franco. In 1937 he published more stories, *To Have And Have Not;* in 1938 Hemingway published *The Fifth Column And The First Forty-Nine Stories* — a volume containing the title play, and all the stories of his previous collections, in addition to seven published but uncollected tales. He wrote in 1940 a novel about the Spanish Civil War, *For Whom The Bell Tolls,* which had great success. Divorced again that year, he married Martha Gellhorn in 1940.

LATER LIFE: Hemingway eagerly looked forward to action in World War II: he maintained an anti-submarine patrol in Cuban waters and planned to decoy submarines with his own boat. Obviously restless in Cuba, where he had settled after 1940, Hemingway went again as a war correspondent to France where he organized a group of irregulars. For example, he entered Paris among the first in August of 1944 and "liberated" the Ritz Hotel where he posted a guard with the notification: "Papa took good hotel. Plenty stuff in cellar." His third marriage ended in divorce in 1944 and he married Mary Welsh. "Papa" Hemingway also had three children from his four marriages: John by the first; Patrick and Gregory by the second. After the war, Hemingway published *Across The River And Into The Trees,* a novel about World War II, which was bitterly attacked by the critics. However, in 1952, he wrote *The Old Man And The Sea,* a story generally acclaimed as one of his finest. He survived an airplane crash in 1954, the year he received the Nobel Prize in Literature. His injuries had taken their toll, and Hemingway died of a "self-inflicted gunshot wound" on July 2, 1961 in his home at Ketchum, Idaho.

THE SUN ALSO RISES: In 1954 the President of the Swedish Academy upon awarding the Nobel Prize to Ernest Hemingway summed up the themes and ideas for which the American writer was being honored: "a heroic pathos which forms the basic element in his awareness of life . . . a natural admiration of every individual who fights the good fight in a world of reality overshadowed by violence and death . . . the bearing of one who is put to the test and who steels himself to meet the cold cruelty

of existence without by so doing repudiating the great and gener-
ous moments. . . . He is one of the great writers of our time,
one of those who, honestly and undauntedly, reproduces the
genuine features of the hard countenance of the age." In his
major novels, *A Farewell To Arms, The Sun Also Rises,* and
For Whom The Bell Tolls, Hemingway interprets man's fate as
he faces a particular problem of "the hard countenance of the
age." In *The Sun Also Rises,* the problem is that of the "lost
generation" — the youth who fought in World War I and are
unable to adjust to the demands of the following decade, the
twenties, as a result of their traumatic experiences.

THE "LOST GENERATION": When Hemingway used Gertrude
Stein's remark that "You are all a lost generation" in the frontispiece of *The Sun Also Rises* as one of the two sources for his
inspiration, he was calling attention to his own situation. After
his exploits in the first World War, Hemingway was unable to
return to a prosaic and ordered life in the United States. He
could not settle down and like Jake Barnes, also a newspaperman
and a war casualty, seek in activity and diversity some cure for
the loss of faith and idealism. Like several others, he became an
expatriate, someone who preferred to live and work outside his
native country. Although one is uncertain and rather dubious
about the potential achievements of Hemingway's cast of characters in *The Sun Also Rises,* no such stigma need be attached
to the merits of the young writers who flocked to Paris after
World War I. In such a heady intellectual and artistic atmosphere
lived F. Scott Fitzgerald, T. S. Eliot, Ezra Pound, and others.
The contributions of the Americans during this period of the
twenties produced one of the flowerings of American literature.

Rather ironically, Hemingway is sketching a group of self-exiles
who will probably not contribute much to the arts although
some of them are trying to write; they are easily diverted by
pleasures, their own malaise, and unfortunate backgrounds. In

this sense, the phrase, "lost generation," would apply not to the rejection of past ideals, political, social, and cultural, which marked Hemingway and his companions in Paris, but to the complete disillusionment with life. These members of the "lost generation" are totally rootless; they have fought and fought well for their countries during the recent war and now have been found useless in a peacetime world. They are naturally embittered at the treatment received for having risked their lives in combat, and they have decided individually to enjoy each day as it comes. It is perhaps easy to criticize these individuals unless one has actually suffered and agonized as they have, and Hemingway sought in *A Farewell To Arms* to show the hardships and effects of war upon men.

THE HEMINGWAY HERO: Hemingway very significantly also quotes below the sentence of Gertrude Stein, in the frontispiece of *The Sun Also Rises,* an excerpt from Chapter One of Ecclesiastes, a pessimistic commentary on man's tragedy, that is to say, his short span of life: "One generation passeth away, and another generation cometh; but the earth abideth forever . . . The sun also ariseth, and the sun goeth down, and hasteth to the place where he arose . . . The wind goeth toward the south, and turneth about unto the north; it whirleth about continually, and the wind returneth again according to his circuits. . . . All the rivers run into the sea; yet the sea is not full; unto the place from whence the rivers come, thither they return again." Thus, life is transitory and kaleidoscopic; nothing man does can stay the passage of time.

How then should man conduct himself under these circumstances? If life is futile and death awaits a person as the inevitable cost of the gift of existence, man must evolve a code. There is no possible victory but there must not be an accepted defeat; man must suffer in silence. Those who are suffering can help each other in the lonesome endeavor to survive. There is no trace of sentimentalism, overt emotionalism, or self-pity on the hero's part; there is also a love of the outdoors, the primitive, and the company of fellow men. This is the world of the "he-man" or "manly manliness." However, the fears and unhappiness are revealed in the dark, which the hero avoids; the exercise of rituals, such as work, company, and action; and the suppression of the will.

Robert Cohn is the "villain" of the novel because he is the opposite of the "Hemingway Hero." It is ironic that on the surface he is more "manly" than the other characters; in Hemingway's view, he represents the problems of American youth who are mature physically but not psychologically. The fact that Cohn is Jewish should not be interpreted as an anti-Semitic element in Hemingway's novel; on the contrary, the author is attempting to picture the causes of Cohn's inability to accept life as it is and his compensatory devices to prove his "All-American" traits.

STYLE: Hemingway's style has been the center of increasing critical attention, favorable and unfavorable, and his message to be read on receipt of the Nobel Prize contained this analysis of his intentions: ". . . For a true writer each book should be a new beginning, where he tries again for something that is beyond attainment. He should always try for something that has never been done, or that others have tried and failed. Then sometimes, with great luck, he will succeed. How simple the writing of literature would be if it were only necessary to write in another way what has been well written. It is because we have made such great writers in the past that a writer is driven far out past where he can go, out to where no one can help him." There is no doubt that Hemingway sought a stylistic break with the past and rejected the flowery and descriptive language of the nineteenth century British and American novel. Hemingway worked with great care and revised constantly; he admitted in an interview with George Plimpton, which was published in *The Paris Review,* that he had always wanted to be a writer but that writing came hard. When questioned about the technical problems involved, he replied in typical Hemingway abbreviated prose that what stumped him was "getting the words right."

Nevertheless, there are certain evidences of Hemingway's stylistic endeavors which should be observed carefully in the reading of *The Sun Also Rises.* Dialogue is the preferred means of communication and description; the dialogue is conversational, in brief sentences or phrases, and the speaker is not directly indicated. At times, the novel resembles a dramatic form rather than the novelistic genre. Hemingway can be lyrical and extended when he wishes to convey his strong feelings about the bullfight ritual, the beauty of nature when man appreciates it, and the daily living of people who are uncorrupted by false values. One should note in particular the episodes in Spain where Hemingway is more expansive. Nevertheless, there is an economy of words, a simple syntax, and an elementary vocabulary with the repetition of key words — all these characteristics reflect Hemingway's training as a journalist. One of his recent critics, Philip Young, admitted that Hemingway's view may be limited and constricted because of the compact and bare style but concludes that "And so I must agree with the Nobel people. The citation was proper, however belated. For me Hemingway is, next to Thoreau, the greatest prose stylist in our literature. That's at the most. At the very least, he is the writer of some of the cleanest, freshest, subtlest, most brilliant and most moving prose of our time. There are passages in three of the four novels I have mentioned here, and in a few of his stories, that can never go bad."

A CRITICAL ANALYSIS OF
THE SUN ALSO RISES

The background tonality of *The Sun Also Rises* is the permanent self-renewing aspect of the earth which remains constant even as it changes, with neither a beginning nor an end in the sight of man. Against this background continuity, Hemingway has drawn the figure of man in all his transience and bewilderment, hemmed in by his birth into a world he never made and a death he does not ask for, but toward which he must inexorably move. This basic juxtaposition of earth and man is stated in the passage from Ecclesiastes from which the book takes its title, that eloquent cry of the prophet as he views the tragedy of man's brief existence in the world: "One generation passeth away, and another generation cometh; but the earth abideth forever. . . . The sun also ariseth, and the sun goeth down, and hasteth to the place whence he arose," as eternal as the wind that "returneth again according to his circuits," and the rivers that return from "whence the rivers come."

But the novel is not merely a despairing cry for man's impermanence. Rather, the state of man is taken as one of the preconditions with which man must come to terms in coming to terms with himself. But death, in all its forms, is not all that man—and Hemingway's man in particular—must face and hold against; for all about him and before him is the rest of humanity, engaged in the same struggle, and in that struggle, engaging also with him. For if man's struggle is not to be entirely solitary, he must also have the company of other human beings. Yet while he desires and needs the solace of their company—and whenever possible, their communion—he must also contend with their conflicts and desires and with the feelings that they, in turn, elicit from him. And in addition to all of this, there is man's confrontation with the consequences of the struggle that has gone on before him, the struggle that we record as history.

THE WAR: Thus, in *The Sun Also Rises* we have the background of the land and the weather, mountain, wind and river; we have the people of the story who represent many kinds of approaches to life; and we have the First World War—in that time, The War—which has established certain basic considerations of their lives.

The War is only mentioned directly a few times in the novel but it is ever-present in the power of its effect upon the individuals who people the book; all the characters are suffering because of the war, directly or indirectly: Jake has been physically emasculated; Lady Brett Ashley has lost her "true love"; and Cohn has not realized the importance of that conflict upon his own generation. Those who have been immediately involved go through the most anguish and rely upon each other for support; in this connection, Jake and Brett complement each other perfectly. Their agony is impenetrable to the comprehension of others. Cohn is still the idealistic and romantic young man that Jake Barnes might have been before he went to war. There is an implied dilemma in Cohn's maladjustment: without the war experience, he has been unable to grow up or mature; with the war experience, he might have been as saddened and disillusioned as Jake Barnes. But above all, The War is implicit in the characters' approach to life, which reflects an outlook which, although it existed before The War, was made concrete in the aftermath. This outlook holds that there are no guidelines, no rules for life.

There is not even such a thing as human nature. As Sartre puts it, "Man is nothing else but what he makes of himself."

A HARD CREED: But while this may be a desirable, if demanding, creed to one who has been brought up believing it, it is another matter for Hemingway's characters. For they had been brought up before the war, when Western society was still giving lip-service, if not credence, to the idea that a demanding but benevolent God did exist, and that there was such a thing as human nature. Therefore there was not only an ideal and a reason for existence, but there was a standard of conduct which men could follow. The terribleness of The War and the exposure of the moral dissolution of society which it brought about, seemed to Hemingway's generation to expose the ideas of the society as illusions. Having nothing, no code, no belief, which would serve in the stead of these ideas, the post-war generation found itself morally afloat, with each man having to create his own ideal and rules of conduct. This is the meaning of "the lost generation" in Hemingway's work: not the generation that is lost in the sense that it is ruined and destroyed (although many were emotionally or physically destroyed in consequence) but the generation that is unable to find the way.

The understanding of the nature of this "lostness" is essential to a true understanding of *The Sun Also Rises*. We can turn to Sartre for a further illumination of this idea when he refers to it as "forlornness," which, he says, follows when we understand that "God does not exist and we have to face all the consequences of this." This is very different from the simple idea of atheism which holds that while God does not exist per se, the norms of honesty, progress and humanism can still be considered as having an *a priori* existence (ideas valid without proof). For Sartre, as for Hemingway, it is nowhere "written that the Good exists, that we must be honest, that we must not lie," and consequently, "man is forlorn, because neither within him nor without does he find anything to cling to."

STARTING FROM SCRATCH: This is Hemingway's "lost" generation and the generation and time of the characters in *The Sun Also Rises*. Thus the characters are not merely portrayals of reckless, profane, and dissipated people, as they have been viewed by some critics. Instead, they constitute a kind of modern version of original man, man starting again from scratch. As such, they assume a certain heroic proportion, and as such they are bound to fall far short of any recognizable ideal. What is heroic about the characters in the novel is the extent to which they try to establish, each for himself, some mode of existence which fulfills their *own* vision of good. In fact, the book is clearly divided between those characters —like Jake Barnes—who have the courage, first, to see that they are forlorn, and second, to struggle to achieve a way of life that is honorable in the midst of their forlornness, and the characters—like Robert Cohn—who do not have the courage, who live in illusion and act upon it.

This, then, is the code. It was Hemingway's own and it is the code of *The Sun Also Rises*: man must establish his own value by facing reality courageously and by acting honestly in terms of that reality. There is no alternative. The rightness of this code is also the thesis of the book. The idea or belief of which the book is proof. Jake Barnes, Bill Gorton, and Pedro Romero hold to the code, and though they are faced with their own difficulties, their existence does not wreak destruction upon others. They are able to work, to create, and to remain independent and responsible. Robert Cohn, and to a lesser degree, Mike Campbell do not hold to the code, and they hurt others and live like dependent children on the bounties of their families.

In this scale, Brett Ashley hangs in the balance: she is realistic, but until the end, she does not act on her own responsibility but out of desire and she wreaks havoc wherever she goes. However, much of the territory of Brett's character lies in ideas which are not outside of, but apart from the code, for she also represents woman and her connection with the earth, an aspect we shall discuss below. Nevertheless, her courageous acceptance of the facts of life indicates that in the *final* balance she belongs to the heroes; and in the end her renunciation of Pedro Romero on the basis of the understanding of the realities of their relationship tips the scales in her favor. But Hemingway's thesis holds.

THE MEANS OF THE NOVEL: The power and vitality of the novel lies partly in this fundamentally moral approach, and it is sustained by the brilliance of Hemingway's writing: the story, the characterization, the subtle echoes of universal themes and images, the precise use of setting, the establishment of mood, and the live quality of the language. The clarity of the descriptive passages; the precision and immediacy of the dialogue which at once gives substance to and illuminates the characters; and the establishment of tone which carries the changes of mood; all these combine to give the book an experiential quality which the years have not softened.

One of the elements which give the book its depth, is, as we have noted, Hemingway's use of certain universal themes and images which have appeared in mythology and various works of literature. But before we look at some of these, it is important to note that the novel does not represent or reflect the development of a single myth, as, for example, does Joyce's *Ulysses*. Instead of adapting a myth to his own ends, Hemingway developed his own way of using it which returns the images it contains to their original meaning and does not require that the reader make use of literary references for their apprehension. Rather, he picked and chose those fragments of ideas which would enhance and clarify the moment of the novel with which he was concerned. However, for our purpose—the deeper understanding of the novel as a work of art—it will be useful to see how those images reflect their earlier use, and how their earlier use enhances these images in the novel. There are two underlying sets of images which are particularly strong in this respect, and these we will discuss.

ECHOES OF "THE WASTELAND":   The first set constitute those elements which echo elements of T. S. Eliot's "The Wasteland," which preceded *The Sun Also Rises* by only four years. It does not matter whether Hemingway used these elements consciously or unconsciously, or even whether he was aware of "The Wasteland" at all (although he had read it). What is important is that he and Eliot used images and ideas in a common context and held, to some extent, similar views of their time, so that our understanding of their common images can be enhanced by the comparison.

As whole works, both use the idea of a protagonist who is physically sterile, which both sets him apart from the world and forces him to be a passive observer of its sexual encounters. We have therefore a parallel between Jake Barnes and Tiresias, the blind hermaphrodite God who can yet see all that goes on between men and women throughout eternity. Eliot says of Tiresias that although he is a spectator, he "is yet the most important personage in the poem, uniting all the rest. . . . What Tiresias *sees,* in fact, is the substance of the poem." Further, all the sexual relations between the characters in the novel seem to have that same neutral quality that the sexual relations in the poem exhibit: "a welcome of indifference." There is also a similarity between the passage of "the hyacinth girl" in the poem and the part in the novel where Jake and Brett are alone in the taxi. Brett's desire, which in the poem appears as an image of a girl coming "late, from the Hyacinth garden/(With her) arms full, and (her) hair wet," meets her lover's impotence. This is expressed in the poem as "I could not/Speak, and my eyes failed, and I was neither/Living nor dead," and in the novel: "there's not a damn thing we could do."

JAKE AS FISHER KING: But the central character in the Wasteland" is also seen as the Fisher King, while Jake Barnes is an ardent fisherman. This similarity is probably not fortuitous. In the legends from which the image of the Fisher King derives and from which Eliot avowedly took the substance of his poem, the Fisher King is sick, and his sickness is reflected in the state of his country, which has become a wasteland. But aside from being a maimed hero in a wasteland, Jake's parallel with the Fisher king illuminates another aspect of his role in the novel, an aspect which can best be elucidated by turning to Eliot's source for his idea: Jessie Weston's *From Ritual to Romance*. The Fisher King, she writes, "is not merely a deeply symbolic figure," associated with the fish as the symbol of life, "but the essential centre . . . a being semi-divine, semi-human, standing between his people and the land, and the unseen forces which control their destiny." While Jake is far from fulfilling this idea in any literal way, he does personify the one individual in the novel who consciously is struggling toward an inner resolution of the modern human condition. And certainly, in terms of the ideas we have already discussed, Jake is a heroic figure. He is one whose struggles and meager resolutions become the basis on which future generations can build toward a stronger approach to reality, toward a sounder humanity which will make the modern wasteland fertile again. In this sense, of course, all heroes are Fisher Kings, but for Hemingway, who tried not only to write, but to live up to his ideal of constant honesty and confrontation with life, the underlying importance of the symbol may have particular validity.

Before we leave "The Wasteland" we can also note some other similarities and echoes which appear in the novel. Like "The Wasteland," the book begins in the spring, a time of "mixing memory and desire." There is also the separation between the mountains—"there you feel free," says Eliot, and that is where Jake and Bill have their moment of peace—and the lower country of city and town where the wasteland is evident. There are also numerous small analogies of detail. For example, one might relate the Stetson of the poem with Bill Gorton matching the sacrificial buried dog of the poem and Bill's joking about the stuffed dog, backed by his comment that, "That was in another country. And besides all the animals were dead." But these details, while of a piece with the theme, are not necessary at this point, for the reader can find them out himself.

THE CENTRAL FEMININE: Another central figure whose significance can be most clearly seen in terms of symbolism is that of Lady Brett Ashley, the sole important feminine character of the story. Certainly the wealthy, distraught female figure of "The Wasteland" bears some resemblance to Brett. There is some of Brett's restlessness in the lady's ramblings in the poem: "My nerves are bad tonight. Yes, bad. Stay with me. . . . What shall I do now? What shall I do? . . . What shall we ever do?" There is also her resolution in sexuality: "I shall rush out as I am, and walk the street/With my hair down, so!" And as the lady plays chess to fill the vacuum, so Brett drinks, continuously, mechanically. But these are only echoes. There are more solid means through which we can gain insight into Brett's role in the novel, and these lie in the novel itself. One clear clue appears when we learn that Robert Cohn calls Brett "Circe." "He claims she turns men into swine," says Mike Campbell, specifying her correspondence to the goddess in Homer's *Odyssey*. But we cannot follow through any analogy between that episode in the Odyssey and any part of the novel.

Brett is the dark goddess, allied with the primitive forces of man, and in this role it is inevitable that she will come together with Romero, who deals with these forces in the form of the bulls. Brett is the *femme fatale par excellence,* the eternal female whom no man can resist. But there is more to Brett than myth and symbol, for she is an individual in her own right, taking her place among the heroes of the story, and it is to the nature of the hero in this novel that we must now turn.

THE HERO: The hero of the story, Jake Barnes, is typical of all Hemingway heroes in that he lives, or struggles to live by a certain code which he has set out for himself: it is of his own making. We can easily list some of the hero's specific characteristics:

1. A fatalistic acceptance of the difficulties of one's life.
2. To "play along and not make trouble for people."
3. Avoidance of self-pity.
4. The use of some form of private ritual by which anxiety is handled.
5. Giving in to despair only in private or in the company of another member of the breed.
6. Ability to recognize and establish an immediate understanding with another member of the breed.
7. A constant struggle to see things exactly as they are, no matter how difficult, rather than as one might wish them to be.
8. Viewing others with as little condemnation as possible, and whenever possible, looking at others with "irony and pity."

All these characteristics can be applied to Jake Barnes, but the ideal of the hero can be most clearly seen in his antithesis, in the anti-hero, Robert Cohn.

The antithesis between Cohn and Jake is drawn sharply and acidly; in fact, so much so that some critics have concluded that Hemingway may have had a particular enemy in mind. For it is an accepted fact that the characters whom Hemingway portrays in the novel are based on actual people he knew in the Left-bank cafés, while the character of Pedro Romero is a projection of Nino de la Palma, a famous matador of the time. A confirmation of the identities of the characters in real life can be found in Harold Loeb's *The Way It Was*.

BILL GORTON: In contrast to Robert Cohn, Bill Gorton stands as another embodiment of the hero, a sort of quiet, less sharply seen reflection of Barnes himself. He too, we gradually realize, despairs of making any sense out of life, but he too does not complain. Instead of finding everything bitter, he calls everything "just wonderful." At first the reader may take him at his word, but after his description of the attack on the Negro prizefighter we realize its meaning, or its meaninglessness. In a sense, Bill's use of the word wonderful is a correlative of Sartre's notion of the absurd.

Bill's membership among the heroic is also expressed in the novel through his ability to communicate wordlessly with Jake and the others of his kind.

Still another aspect of the hero, both in *The Sun Also Rises* and in the other Hemingway works, is his freedom from bondage to women. This does not mean that he cannot love a woman, or that he does not desire her, but that he cannot, to use a common phrase, become wrapped around a woman's little finger. Nor, for that matter, can he be dominated by one. Cohn, on the other hand, is a man who is not free of woman. Remembering the bookish basis of Cohn's ideal man, it is likely that Hemingway intended to imply that Cohn's vision of masculinity was identified with sexual virility, and that the proof of masculinity lay in the proof of the latter. While this is a well-known psychological type, what we are concerned with here is that this misapprehension of the nature of virility —which to Hemingway lies in courage, not potency—typifies the Hemingway *anti*-hero, not the hero himself. We may note further, that it is this misunderstanding that has led many critics and some of the public to view the Hemingway hero as a kind of hairy-chested Don Juan, when in reality this image is the embodiment of his opposite.

BRETT AND THE CODE: It is in terms of the code, of the heroic standard, that Brett also appears as raised above the dangerous and magical depths of her womanhood. Her virtues are those of the Hemingway ethic, except, being a woman, she cannot exercise the self-control required by it. She is until the end at the mercy of her desire. Her ritual to still her inner anguish is not private, but requires another for its execution, and thus she injures others. But in all other respects (as we can see if we view the list we have made), she conforms to the code, and like all those who do, she is immediately recognizable as one of those who belong. And in the end, Brett's inherent qualities are manifest in a heroic act, when she sends Romero away realizing that she could do nothing but lead him to emotional and professional ruin. The importance of the right act that is performed of one's own volition, from one's own conviction as to what is right, is underscored here by Hemingway.

GOD AND GOOD: Despite the fact that for the heroic individual God is not, the matter of religion is a live concern in the novel. For as we noted earlier, the hero does not merely erase the concept of God from his picture of the universe, but removes the idea of an *a priori* human nature as well. Sartre plumbs the importance of this distinction in terms of the existentialist, who, he says, "thinks it very distressing that God does not exist, because all possibility of finding values in a heaven of ideas disappears along with Him; there can no longer be an *a priori* Good, since there is no infinite and perfect consciousness to think it. . . . Indeed, everything is permissible if God does not exist." And Sartre's regret is shared by Jake from the same point of view. It would be so simple, Hemingway implies, to handle one's anguish and fear through a formal religious, rather than a difficult private ritual, so pleasant to find solace in the beautiful churches with their "wonderful big windows" and the smell of incense, to have faith in a caring God.

GOOD AND VALUE: Jake and the others of his kind look within their own lives for a basis of value, and it is Jake's struggle to determine the nature of values that he can live by that appears most clearly in the book. Value, Jake recognizes, is the fundamental coin of the moral world among human beings.

While this statement of value is set in commercial terms, these belie the importance of the concept in the hero's life. For if there is no God, and no rule of right conduct, there is only oneself, and one's responsibility for one's acts, and of course, for one's life. And what is a good life? While the specifics differ for each man, the basic tenor is clear to Hemingway: it is a life that does not bring trouble to others and it is a life that one finds good oneself. How does one attain that life? By choosing what is valuable and obtaining it. But, this of course presumes that one recognizes what is valuable to oneself and adheres to that standard.

A GREEK-AMERICAN VIEW: This aspect of the novel is illuminated further in an exchange with Count Mippipopolous. Now that he has learned from life what is valuable, no act of fortune or of another individual will change his understanding of those values. In other words, having chosen his values honestly, he will not descend to the dishonesty of bitterness which would turn them into sour grapes. Perhaps he might say that love means certain things to him, but cannot come before everything. He would not lose himself in love; lose, like Cohn, his dignity, his value of himself. Thus love might have a place in his values in relation to other values he holds, and which he lives by. Although the Count in the novel is a delightful author's set piece, he provides us with an important insight into the practical side of Hemingway's philosophy.

THE BULLFIGHT: The community of the heroic is seen in another aspect through the medium of the bullfight—its protagonists, and its *aficionados*— and through this important medium we are also brought into a deeper insight into the nature of the hero as Jake Barnes.

Before we proceed to examine the significance of bullfighting in Pamplona, it will be useful to consider the significance underlying the bullfight itself. As the fish has been (and still is) a universal symbol of life, so the bull has been (and remains) a universal symbol of death. But it is not death in the simple sense of an end to life. Rather it is death as an aspect of all the dark, powerful forces of nature which at once are the source of all life's energy and the means of its destruction. Within man, the bull represents the dark urges, which unless they are transformed into those passions and desires which we accept as the finer attributes of man, appear as lust, rage, and a drive toward the destruction of oneself and of others. Psychologically, the equivalent of the bull is the id, the undifferentiated life force in human beings. But it is important to remember, particularly in the understanding of the bullfights in the novel, that the bull is not merely negative. Untransformed, unconquered, untamed, he is dangerous, as is the untransformed, uncontrolled bull in man. But in conquering the bull within, man reaches to his greatest heights, for then he can combine the great power of the bull with the vision of his consciousness, and become a kind of super-man.

THE BULL CULTS: This idea, and its enactment, underlay the ancient bull cults which once were to be found around the world. Using the primitive idea that an enactment in physical reality would bring about the corresponding inner event, men who wished to join in the mysteries of such cults would engage in combat with real bulls. The Greek story of Theseus and the Minotaur is now generally acknowledged to be a description of such a ritual. And it is from those rituals that what we know today as the modern bullfight has descended in a direct line. Even today, the bullfight is surrounded with ritual, both for the participants and for the spectators.

There is one other element that is important, and that is the aspect of transference, between the matador and the spectators. For underlying the idea of the bullfight as a public spectacle lies the notion that the matador's engagement with the bull is *shared* by the spectators. On the one hand, he dares and does what each individually cannot do: he kills the bull *in fact* in accordance with prescribed ritual, with courage and with honor and with respect for the true nature of the bull. Since the people are one with the matador, they too, kill the bull, but it is their own "bull" that dies, and dies nobly. Yet at the same time that the matador kills the bull for them, they give him their combined strength, and it is with their power, combined with his skill, by which the deed is done. This was the original purpose of the bullfight proper—that in the fight which preceded the killing of the bull the hypnotic beauty of the matador's movements would provide "the way in" to the moment in which the matador and his people were one.

MORE THAN EXISTENCE: Understanding these unspoken elements, we can now approach the fiesta in Pamplona and its significance to Jake with better understanding. The trip to Pamplona is for Jake a kind of pilgrimage, and as such, it sheds new light on the man in the novel. For we have seen Jake thus far as an existentialist character who might have been in one of Sartre's works. But although Hemingway seems to have accepted the existentialist ethic, and most of its premises, he yet seems to have believed in a deeper bond between man and nature, and among like men, than the modern existentialist philosophy would allow. While God is dead, and a pre-existing humanistic ideal is an illusion, there is yet a bond between man and the earth which could, under certain conditions, be experienced, and that experience is essentially mystical. Accordingly, his hero, Jake, appears in some unspoken way to be aware of this experience and goes to seek it out.

On the surface then, this should be grounds for establishing another connection between Jake and Brett, for both find their fulfillment in what can be viewed as a pagan ceremony. But

this is not altogether true. Brett's paganism is ecstatic, Diony-
sian, based on the idea that a mystic communion can be
achieved through self-abandonment. Jake's "paganism" is the
exact opposite: as in the bullfight, communion is achieved by
a carefully maintained control whose stages are the stages of
the ritual. And every aspect of the bullfight is surrounded
with ritual.

THE AFICIONADO: One of the first aspects of the bullfight to which Hemingway introduces us is the concept of the
aficionado. The aficionado, Hemingway explains to us, is one
who is *passionate* about bullfights, and this passion forms, like
the heroic standard to which it belongs (or possibly, which
belongs to it) a bond of understanding among its adherents.
As Hemingway describes the way this bond is made manifest,
we find that we are apprehending something which has the
quality of a mystic ritual, including the sacred touch, or
blessing, which so many religious rituals have in common.

There is also a passage which seems to underline Hemingway's awareness of the original significance of the bullfight,
and which unites the idea of the *aficionado* with membership
in a kind of bull cult, in which Jake says that Montoya "always
smiled as though bullfighting were a very special secret between us. . . . It would not do to expose it to people who
would not understand." In the light of this total acceptance,
the importance of Montoya's rejection of Jake as an accom-
plice in the union of Brett and Romero can be understood.

THE DESENCAJONADA: The first event, or ritual, for
the *aficionado* attending a bullfight is the *desencajonada,* the
arrival (or literally, the unloading) of the bulls. In the *desencajonada* in the novel we get our first glimpse of the bull himself, and the full power and majesty of the animal—which must
be appreciated to apprehend the power of the bullfight itself
—is made evident to the reader in one of the most brilliant
moments of writing in the book. Here, in the writing itself,
is the full symbol of the bull in all its power.

One of the most important preliminary rituals to a bullfight is the preparation of the matador, and even today this tends to be conducted in a fairly solemn manner. It consists primarily of dressing the matador in his special clothes which are specific to his role and particularly noted for the fineness of their detail and their tightness. This may possibly reflect the fact that the "matadors" of the ancient bull cults were usually naked, but often painted and decorated with intricate designs.

PEDRO ROMERO: In the fiesta section of *The Sun Also Rises,* Romero becomes an alternate for Jake as he stands out in contrast to the anti-hero, Cohn. Romero, like Jake, is everything that Cohn is not, only more so. If we did not know it before, we learn it then: Romero is one of the elect.

Romero is uncorrupted by the mood of the "lost generation"; and he has none of the anguish which besets the modern man of the wasteland, Jake and his party. As the critic Melvin Blackman notes: "With the instinctive sureness of a primitive who need never question his reason for living, he pursued his natural course. And it was this which even Brett came to recognize. There was an absolute center to him. He did not have to drink, he did not have to keep running away. His inner core was brought into a vital, active relationship with life. As Jake commented, it is only a bullfighter who lives life to the hilt, bringing to his work all his courage, intelligence, discipline, and art."

THE FINAL OUTCOME: Many critics have viewed the novel as representing a cycle of existence which returns upon itself, ending as it began, in keeping with the theme of the earth's cyclical character stated in the prefaced quotation from Ecclesiastes. For example, Philip Young holds that in the final section of the novel, "a solitary Jake, rehabilitating himself, washes away his hangover in the ocean. Soon, it is all gone, he is returned to Brett as before, and we discover that we have come full circle, like all the rivers, the winds, and the sun, to the place where we began." In a similar vein, Max

Hertzberg writes: "The fact that nothing really leads anywhere in the novel points to its central theme; the action
comes full circle to imitate the sun, which, as described in
Ecclesiastes, also rises only to hasten to the place where it
arose." But if one rereads Hemingway's quotation from the
prophet, we realize that while the aspect of unbroken continuity is characteristic of the *earth, man's* life is not self-re-
turning, but terminal. Hemingway himself said that the novel
was not "a hollow or bitter satire, but a damn tragedy with
the earth abiding forever as the hero."

The closing lines of the book are often quoted to support the
cyclical theory of the novel, and it is true that they super-
ficially reflect the first exchange between Brett and Jake in the
book. But if one looks closely, there is a great difference. The
tone is completely different, and so is the meaning of the
words. We can see the distance that Brett has come from the
time when Jake's touch would turn her "all to jelly." It is as
if the violence of her affair with Romero had erased her physical bondage to a man with whom she could not be physically
united. In a like manner, Jake has changed.

BUT STILL TRAGEDY: This does not presuppose that Brett,
or Jake, or any of the other characters will change their mode
of existence or find freedom from their despair. Rather it reflects the idea discussed earlier, that the hero struggles constantly to confront the truth and to live by it, and to derive
from his struggle a measure of value by which he can live
still more honestly. Certainly this falls short of the ideal of
the traditional hero who is totally transformed by his experience and appears as a new man. But this would not have been
in keeping with Hemingway's measure of truth, a measure he
took from life itself. As in real life, one learns from one's experience, not all at once, but bit by bit. "Perhaps," as Jake
says, "as you went along you did learn something." But further,
Hemingway believed that one could only learn if one faced
the truth unflinchingly. Thus to learn even "something" re-

quired a heroic effort. This Jake has done, and his courage, and his reward—however meager it may seem by more romantic standards—must be contrasted against Cohn's cowardice and his total failure in his own confrontation with reality.

Nevertheless, the book is a tragedy, because even the greatest courage does not enable the characters to rise above their circumstances, but only enables them to learn "how to live in it." That is the best man can do in the face of a bitter reality, and the best is what Jake and Brett and Bill Gorton have done.

A GLANCE AT STYLE: The beauty and fitness of the language and style of *The Sun Also Rises* has often been commented on at length. Here we will only note briefly a few of its aspects.

There is the basic simplicity of line which Hemingway attains primarily by the use of simple and compound, rather than complex sentences; the minimization of adjectives; and a preference for Anglo-Saxon rather than latinized words. The dialogue echoes the rhythms of natural speech, but while it is realistic, it is not clinical. Hemingway's achievement can be viewed as a balance between the aesthetically detached and rarified language of Henry James and the frank reproduction of daily speech used in the works of many contemporary writers. For all his simplicity and directness, Hemingway is the master of allusion, of conveying feeling and situation by nuance. At the same time, when the context demands it, he can be completely explicit, as for example, when he etches the setting through which the people and the bulls run on their way to the bull-ring in Pamplona.

But perhaps Hemingway's greatest stylistic achievement is his ability to achieve emotion through his simple line. Throughout the novel Hemingway manages to let the reader not only see what Jake sees at the moment, but also *feel* what Jake feels—without *telling* the reader what that feeling is. We observed an excellent example when we discussed the meaning of Jake's confrontation with the weeping Cohn. At all times, it was Hemingway's concern to achieve this emotion, and there is a note on his effort in this respect which appears in the opening passages of another of his works. There he says that he "found the greatest difficulty, aside from knowing truly what you really felt, rather than what you were supposed to feel, and had been taught to feel, was to put down what really happened in action."

THE SUN ALSO RISES

BOOK ONE

Chapters I-VII

CHARACTER ANALYSES

JAKE BARNES: He is the narrator of the story who gradually reveals himself in the first book. Until his meeting with Brett, Jake is more interested in explaining the situation of Robert Cohn. The reader is early made cognizant that something is wrong with Jake; the indications are fairly evident that he is incapable of having sexual relations.

JAKE'S LOVE FOR BRETT: Only after the initial meeting with Brett does the reader begin to form for himself a new view of Jake. This vision, nevertheless, alters totally the prevailing picture of a rather morose and withdrawn journalist. Then, the first, clear outlines of the "Hemingway Hero" come into focus: Jake is capable of deep and sorrowful emotions; he is tender, compassionate, thoughtful. He must be a man of action. The irony is that Jake has strong sexual desires which can never be fulfilled. The love between the two is the undercurrent of this first book.

FRIENDSHIP WITH COHN: On the surface, Cohn would appear to be one of Jake's best friends; in the first chapters, Cohn dominates the narration. Indeed, more facts are learned about Cohn than about Jake even though the latter is the narrator and the hero. As the story unfolds, Cohn is unmasked by the author: instead of a pleasant companion, he is the antithesis of Jake. Jake becomes more cognizant of Cohn's boy-man personality in Chapter VI when Frances and her lover argue. Thus, in Book One, Jake has changed from a friend, or at least a tennis companion and listener to Cohn, to a suspicious and increasingly antagonistic acquaintance of his fellow American.

BRETT: Although Brett appears rather late in the novel and is seldom alone with Jake, she begins to dominate the action. At least, the course of the story will revolve a great deal about her, it is clear at this point. Like Jake, Brett wears a mask. Even a woman can follow the "Hemingway Code" and adhere to the ideal of the hero. It is ironic that Jake is more normal, except sexually, than Brett, who is an extreme example of the "lost generation."

ROBERT COHN: In a sense, Robert Cohn controls a great deal of the dialogue and the actions of Book One. Although he belongs to the expatriates, he is removed from them by temperament and by volition. If Jake Barnes is considered as a "Hemingway Hero," then within the same canon, Robert Cohn may be dubbed the "Hemingway Anti-Hero." In fact, the antithesis with Jake Barnes is drawn sharply and bitterly; so much so that critics have concluded that Hemingway may have had a particular enemy in mind. If not, then the author is striving to build up a concept as Mark Spilka writes: "Cohn still upholds a romantic view of life, and since he affirms it with stubborn persistence, he acts like a goad upon his wiser contemporaries. . . . Of course, there is much that is traditional in the satire on Cohn. Like the many victims of romantic literature, from Don Quixote to Tom Sawyer, he lives by what he reads and neglects reality at his own and others' peril." In short, Cohn is fundamentally bewildered by the world of his contemporaries and he does not understand the members of his own generation. He does not belong to the group with which he associates, and Hemingway may be implying that Cohn does not belong in Europe.

COHN'S BACKGROUND: Since Hemingway took the trouble to sketch so many details of Cohn's background, some of the dilemmas in the young man's situation can be seen in the light of the descriptions afforded him. While the fact that Cohn is Jewish cannot be attributed to any anti-Semitic slur on Hemingway's side, nevertheless the author seeks to explicate Cohn against this knowledge.

It also has been pointed out by critics that Hemingway may be suggesting some reasons for his own flight from the United States; he may have seen in the innocent and immature youth of America an inability to cope with reality. Their upbringing, education, and whole set of attitudes were romantic and bookish; they were unprepared to exist on equal terms with men in a world of experienced and hardened individuals. There is no doubt that Hemingway is particularly severe in his critique of Robert Cohn and perhaps significantly he terminates Cohn's appearance in Book One with the angry scene at the end of Chapter VI.

MINOR CHARACTERS: Both Cohn and Frances are examples of an American marriage which fails because both are unrealistic, self-seeking, ambitious and are not actually in love from the beginning. On Hemingway's part, there is another bitter rendition of his attitude on the defeats of American society and mores.

Harvey Stone, although he appears briefly, contributes two ideas of Hemingway to the themes of the novel. He is typical of the impoverished young American in Paris—witty, frank, and lazy—whom Hemingway must have met many times. However, Harvey Stone foreshadows the growing tensions with Cohn that Jake and his friends will have; Stone also analyzes briefly but accurately Cohn's juvenile qualities which the author judges as his serious defects. Count Mippipopolous plays a role only in the first book; he is one of the several extraneous characters in this novel as well as others of Hemingway who come on stage briefly, contribute little to the action, and then vanish from the story. However, this technical aspect of Hemingway's art does not imply that the Count is totally without importance; on the contrary, he is also a member of the "lost generation," although older than the others, and exemplifies the manly virtues praised by the novelist. The Count is gentlemanly and enjoys life and values friendship; and he accepts life on its own terms.

The Braddocks are again Hemingway's representation of the wrong type of American in Paris. The few French characters introduced in the first book are perhaps stereotypes of the novelist's impressions of Parisians. It is interesting to note how Hemingway reproduces in dialogue the speech patterns of a native. He attempts to convey the syntax of the foreign language, with the use of the original French, into the context of English. The same procedure will be adhered to in speeches with other Frenchmen and with the Spaniards.

COMMENT

THE "LOST GENERATION":   There is, strictly speaking, no formal "plot" or unfolding of an action in the first book, which comprises nevertheless a fourth of the novel. Hemingway establishes a mood or an atmosphere; for example, he is very precise in his descriptions of Paris not, however, with lengthy passages but with the names of streets, places, and characteristic traits of Parisian life. In short, Hemingway strives to instill a feeling for the beauty of the city and the warmth and humanity of the daily living. In order to make the reader react favorably, he must make him at "home"; he must make him understand why certain Americans rejected residence in the United States and chose Paris. For instance, Hemingway is most attentive to the privacy of the individual in the city; all the characters come and go as they please and lead whatever lives they prefer. There is a comfortable atmosphere in the cafés at which Jake Barnes and his friends stop to eat and drink so often; indeed, these elementary delights are constantly referred to by the novelist. Once the setting is accepted, then, some of the psychological framework of the "lost generation" is more easily penetrated.

Oscar Cargill in his critique of this novel wrote that *"The Sun Also Rises* has no peer among American books that have attempted to take account of the cost of the War upon the morals of the War generation and . . . no better polemics against war than this, which was meant for no polemic at all." All the characters are suffering because of the war, directly or indirectly: Jake has been wounded; Brett lost her lover; and Cohn has not realized the importance of that conflict upon his own generation. Those who have been immediately involved go through the most anguish and rely upon each other for support; in this connection, Jake and Brett complement each other perfectly. Their agony defies comprehension from others. Cohn is still the idealistic and romantic young man that Jake Barnes might have been before he went to war. There is an implied dilemma in Cohn's maladjustment: without the war experience, he has never grown up or matured; with the war experience, he probably would have been as saddened and as disillusioned as Jake Barnes.

LOVE: None of the three characters enjoys love in the first book and yet each is seeking it. Mark Spilka calls this "the death of love" in his essay on the novel: "It serves the same purpose for the expatriate crowd in Paris. In some figurative manner these artists, writers, and derelicts have all been rendered impotent by the war. Thus, as Barnes presents them, they pass before us like a parade of sexual cripples, and we are able to measure them against his own forbearance in the face of a common problem. Whoever bears his sickness well is akin to Barnes; whoever adopts false postures, or willfully hurts others, falls short of his example. This is the organizing prin-

ciple in Book I, this alignment of characters by their stoic
qualities. But, stoic or not, they are all incapable of love, and
in their sober moments they seem to know it." It is also indicated by Hemingway that the cause for this so-called "death
of love" is World War I; and although the past conflict plays
no direct role in the novel, it must be grasped as the central,
forming fact around which the story revolves.

STYLE: *The Sun Also Rises* secured a place in American
literature because of the forceful and original manner in which
it was written. Hemingway admitted in later discussions that
the novel cost him a great deal of time; he wrote and rewrote
in order to polish the deceptively simple style. The author
grants that "movement" is slow although "change" is always
there; life, which is basically slow-paced without rapid and
sudden motions, must be accurately depicted in the novel.
The Sun Also Rises is creating a mood and describing an atmosphere, and the characters are caught within this world
not of their own making.

Hemingway, always vividly cognizant of the artistic struggle,
draws for the reader an interesting and true picture of his
contemporaries during the twenties in Paris. Nevertheless,
there abounds in Book One a restraint that is almost classical;
and despite the rather sordid situations denoted, such as the
case of Lady Brett Ashley, Georgette, Jake Barnes' emascula-
tion, and the unhappy love affair of Frances and Robert Cohn,
the language is not naturalistic. It is conversational and realistic
but it is not clinically detailed; for example, only subtly is one
told about Jake's wounds. If anything, Hemingway has attained
a balance between the aesthetically detached and rarified language of Henry James and the brutally frank and crude expressions of many contemporary writers.

BOOK TWO

Chapters VIII-XIII

CHARACTER ANALYSES

JAKE BARNES: Hemingway never uncovers Jake's world in Paris for the reader; of course, the correspondent apparently works hard at his job but from all indications the job is not especially arduous. As part of the code, the hero must not be loquacious about himself; and Hemingway does nothing to alleviate the mystery by means of the revelations of a third person.

JAKE'S LOVE OF SPAIN: As soon as the "Spanish" phase of the novel starts in Chapter X, there is a very distinct change in Jake Barnes. His love for Paris is far different from his love for Spain because the French capital represents a refuge from the States, the chance to live individually and freely, and the occasion to meet friends conveniently. However, Jake is never ecstatic about Paris; he is objective and detailed and without any disparagement conveys his feeling for the city. Jake feels the intimate contact with nature and an unmechanized existence as he crosses the Spanish frontier. For instance, Hemingway writes glowingly, still with economical style, however, of the trip to Pamplona. He also describes with admiration the setting of Burguete; in fact, the episode of the fishing trip in the mountains has nothing to do with the progress of the novel, properly speaking. Almost like an essay or even a short story, the latter a genre which Hemingway cultivated with extraordinary success, the Burguete diversion exemplifies the "Hemingway Code" and the life which the author himself led. Jake's attraction to the Spanish people is also very markedly indicated; there were no such close ties with the few French individuals of the book although Jake liked them.

THE BULLFIGHT RITUAL: If Hemingway ever becomes lyrical and impassioned in *The Sun Also Rises,* that phenomenon occurs in the several passages about the bullfight. Montoya, the innkeeper, calls Jake Barnes "a real aficionado." The word itself cannot be exactly translated as Hemingway hints; *aficionado* contains more than the meaning of a "fan." An *aficionado* is one who is enamored of the bullfight ritual as Hemingway demonstrated in *Death In The Afternoon* and other instances. The novelist is not only detailed, precise, and accurate in his renditions of the opening ceremonies of the annual festivities in Pamplona; he lengthens his descriptions and savors the full flavor of his knowledge throughout the rest of *The Sun Also Rises.* There is a rising crescendo of interest: in these chapters only the bare indication of the total beauty of the bullfight is brought into light by the scene of the arrival of the bulls.

The "Hemingway Hero" must enjoy the spectacle, and all the participants express their enthusiasm for the sport. All the characters see in the enterprise the confrontation of life with death; the sudden, swift end of the gored steer satisfies their thirst for action as a solution to the boredom and disillusionment they endure. The world of the bullfight is cruel at times as in this introductory maneuver, but this phase of life is realistic, manly, and representative. Hemingway, never a writer to waste words, wished to extract the symbolism of the bullfight as synonymous in many ways with the plight of the "lost generation."

BRETT: Despite her dissipated manners, Brett adheres like the males to the canon of courage, stoicism, and silence about woes which Cohn so crudely ignores. With the exception of Jake, Brett grasps the import of the bullfight ceremonies with enthusiasm; she knows perhaps that there is a hidden meaning for them when she cautiously notes that the bulls do not look "happy." In fact, she is courageous and is not frightened at the sight of the gored steer. It is then of significance that Jake and Brett, the two unknown lovers of the circle, fully appreciate the *fiesta* of Pamplona. Likewise, Brett is proving her loyalty to the "Hemingway Code," and it is unusual that the author would concede this privilege to a female whom he so often sketches with little flattery in his works. Perhaps, as Leslie Fiedler implies, Hemingway praises her because she is so unfeminine: "To yield up her cropped head would be to yield up her emancipation from female servitude, to become feminine rather than phallic; and this Brett cannot do. She cannot become a woman, that is to say, no matter how hard she tries, for Hemingway has imagined her—and for once he has imagined a character who convincingly wills the role he has imposed upon her. She thinks of herself as a flapper, though the word perhaps would not have occurred to her, as a member of the Lost Generation; but the Spaniards know her immediately as a terrible goddess, the avatar of an ancient archetype."

ROBERT COHN: Cohn is sentimental and desires recognition and appreciation, which is forced to the surface in his contacts; the partisans of the "Hemingway Code" are provoked to displeasure and anger by his immaturity. He is bored by the *fiesta* of Pamplona and is constantly critical of the whole procedure; and Hemingway seems to indicate that the bullfight is a ceremony which an American, like Cohn, does not comprehend. Cohn brings to the atmosphere the American air of efficiency and pragmatism, which is beyond the Spanish sport. Cohn in these chapters represents the cloud upon the horizon of the party's happiness, and Hemingway hints that surely more bickering will take place. However, Cohn is usually dubbed as "nice" by the others—except for his offensive behavior. His "nice" qualities are unfortunately never brought to the reader's attention, and the author is more than content in the unsavory portrait he paints of the young man.

BILL GORTON: Of the group, he is probably the most successful; Bill belongs to the "lost generation" in spirit and in sympathy, but he has learned to work hard and adjust to the twenties. In fact, he delivers a good-natured but highly accurate analysis of Jake Barnes' plight and that of the other expatriates during the fishing trip to Burguete. Bill Gorton, at the beginning of Chapter XII, cuts incisively into the heart of the novel's problems in a rare, revelatory confession on Hemingway's part. Bill Gorton, a true member of the "lost generation," is a participant of the two worlds; the world of the present and future is seized by him, and he still retains sympathy and friendship with those who do not enter into the stream of progress.

MONTOYA: According to Hemingway, he is a "good man" because of his honesty, simplicity, and sincerity. He is perhaps a typical figure of the older generation in Spain for Hemingway, someone who has not been transformed by the mores of the twentieth century.

WILSON-HARRIS: · This Englishman is another example of the extraneous character who makes a brief entrance into the novel and has nothing to do with the plot or action. Hemingway values companionship and good fellowship which the Englishman represents.

OTHER MINOR CHARACTERS: There are certain incidents within these chapters which, like individual characters in the vein of Montoya and Wilson-Harris, present figures having nothing to contribute directly to the plot but which expose Hemingway's ideas and themes. For example, Jake and Bill meet two different groups of tourists on the train from Paris to Bayonne in Chapter IX. Both parties illustrate Hemingway's antipathy for some of his own countrymen, or at least his amusement at the prejudices and narrow-mindedness of some Americans.

On the bus trip to Burguete, Jake and Bill chat in English
with an old man who lived in the United States forty years
ago. Thus, the spirit of camaraderie knows no boundaries of
age, nationality, or religion; this would seem to be Hemingway's indirect lesson in the vignette.

COMMENT

BRETT'S LOVERS: By the end of this section, Brett dominates the action such as it is; Jake is the narrator and the
hero but Brett is the far more interesting individual. Stewart
Sanderson writes that "Brett, by contrast, is completely honest
with herself, and honourable, too, in her own fashion. Gone
to the dogs and aware of it, morally broken by cruel experience, she is presented with great compassion. She is the most
real character in the novel: Hemingway has succeeded so
well in presenting Brett as Jake knows her and feels for her
that, when we lay the book aside, we feel we have known her
too, and been moved by the same sympathy for her plight."

THE "FIESTA":   Upon its prior publication in England, this
novel was given the title of *Fiesta,* and the Pamplona residence
is certainly the central descriptive and emotional experience in
Hemingway's work. Stewart Sanderson notes the importance of
the setting: "At Pamplona the real trouble starts. Hemingway
uses the mounting excitement of the *fiesta,* the fireworks, the
drinking and dancing, the running of the bulls, to build up an
atmosphere of tension as a setting for the climax of his tale.
It is a neat bit of craftsmanship, in which critics of the sym-
bolically-minded persuasion have found a happy and reward-
ing hunting-ground." Carlos Baker, the official biographer of
Hemingway and one of the leading "critics of the symbolically-
minded persuasion," warns that Hemingway is an adroit artist
who does not indicate bluntly his intentions: "To borrow a
phrase from Keats, the symbolic in Hemingway's writings must

come as naturally as the leaves to a tree or it had better not come at all. He seems early to have rejected the arbitrary importation of symbols which are not strictly germane to the action in hand, thus agreeing with Coleridge's assertion—though in a way different from what Coleridge meant—that the symbol 'always partakes of the reality which it renders intelligible.' "

The *fiesta* gathers together the clan of friends, and the descriptions provide the warmth and association which the action in Paris did not. Paris is their place of exile, but Pamplona has lessons about life and their participation in the world. It is a touch of irony that the "holiday" is just that: there is no permanence in the seven days of joy, and all must return to their previous hopeless existence. However, Hemingway shows his mastery of style in the sure and exact manner with which he draws this European celebration.

STRUCTURE: There are three distinct divisions in the chapters of this part of Book Two: those that deal with life in Paris and the trip to Pamplona, the fishing trip at Burguete, and the start of the *fiesta* in Pamplona. The scenes in Paris are very reminiscent of the mood already established in Book One, and the companionship of Bill and Jake is likewise similar to the events of the first book. However, once the journey to Spain is started, there is a more evident drive and force in the novel; Jake has been eagerly planning this expedition. For the first time, Hemingway brings nature and somewhat lengthy description into his story when the Spanish border is crossed. A different atmosphere pervades the first glimpses of Pamplona which is not redolent of the more active environment of Paris. Hemingway conveys the idea that life is more slow and measured; Pamplona really does not belong to the modern age as his characters do not either.

The fishing trip to Burguete is the "happiest" interlude in the entire novel and ironically it makes no solid contribution to the plot and to the problems of Brett and her lovers. In fact, the Burguete pages could be omitted completely from the novel without any loss in a plot analysis. The days in Burguete illustrate Hemingway's personal and aesthetic credo for the life of man; and therefore the fishing trip is highly valid for any understanding of his doctrines. Man needs the company of good, congenial friends with like personalities; and he requires the natural life as his true habitat. It is the combination of "man-nature" which marks the Hemingway theory. The two friends chat amiably about trivialities, but a rapport is set up between men in the midst of a sylvan setting. If such influence exists, the Burguete phase denotes the "return to nature" theme from Rousseau, the French philosopher of the eighteenth century, and Thoreau in the nineteenth century with his residence in Walden. In the third structural division at Pamplona, a busy air is immediately noticeable after the calm days in Burguete; but this is still languid after the days in Paris. Hemingway has provided three sites for the exposition of his problem of man in the nineteen twenties: the frenetic pace of a big city, such as Paris, where one may find anonymity; the escapism of an isolated atmosphere in nature at Burguete; and the genteel and traditional ways of Pamplona.

SYMBOLISM: Three symbolic devices stand out in these chapters: the bullfight, the mountains, and the church. The bullfight is the most obvious, and critics, such as Leslie Fiedler, see in this Spanish sport a Freudian interpretation about the love between Brett and her men. At least, the bullfight ceremonies symbolize the struggle of man with death and the futility of life against impersonal forces. The *fiesta* is a symbol of the brief moment of escape they all yearn for in order to forget the past, present, and future. Carlos Baker claims that the mountains always mean the pure and the good life for Hemingway; his characters are happy in the mountains, and the life is undisturbed by the anxieties of personal and social cares. It is interesting to observe that Burguete, that tranquil phase between Paris and Pamplona, is described as being located in the mountains. As Jake and Bill descend into Pamplona, they would be going down to trouble and strife. In a very important paragraph of introspective analysis, and the rarity of such passages in Hemingway adds to the critical weight afforded the words. Jake has sought in vain in religion for values in his agonizing conflict with himself and with life; he finds no solace in religious observance and departs alone and unfortified. One critic has pointed to this characteristic aspect of the Hemingway creations in these words: "Hence Hemingway's naturalism is always promising to break through its isolation and to link up with the world of spirit but the promise is never quite achieved. It is this failure which will weigh heaviest against him in the final summing up. . . . The obliqueness of his characters derives from his refusal or inability (whether he is unconscious or willing captive of his age is a nice question) to give evidence to that potential in man which either raises him above or sinks him below the rest of the animal world." Whether or not one agrees with Michael Moloney in his critique of the failure of religious values in the quest of Hemingway's characters, the fact cannot be denied that the individuals have to stand alone in their search for identity. Of course, if the hero or the others encountered such a convenient answer to their questions, much of Hemingway's thesis would be destroyed. The author is stressing the impact of diverse elements against man—faced at the end by death as the gored steer in these chapters.

BOOK TWO

Chapters XIV-XVIII

CHARACTER ANALYSES

JAKE BARNES: Besides continuing as the narrator, Jake returns to the center of the whole action; this is his show, for which he has planned since the beginning of the novel. For example, Earl Rovit writes that "Jake is both sympathetic and reliable narrator ultimately, but his emergence as a full-fledged, graduating tyro hero is gained only after he has fallen several times, forced himself to admit his failures to himself, and secured his own forgiveness. As we have seen in our previous discussions of Hemingway's fiction, it is the irony of the unsaid that says most clearly and resonantly what the stripped usable values are, and what one has to pay for them." There is a brilliant technical achievement on Hemingway's part at the beginning and at the end of this admittedly arbitrary division of the novel. Jake analyzes his feelings alone in bed in Chapter XIV, the reasons for which are not fully realized until the somber dinner at the end of Chapter XVIII. Ironically, Hemingway concludes Chapter XIII and Chapter XVIII with dinner parties; the two meals are closely related because both gatherings hint at and prove the eventual defeat of any attempt at happiness.

JAKE'S MANLINESS: His defeats in the game of life are the immediate cause for his new maturity. In a sense, all of Hemingway's heroes go through this baptism of fire, in war or in disillusionment, to reach manhood. Ivan Kashkeen defines this

experience as "alive in the midst of death." He explains his
concept thus: "In grappling with these problems, in overcom-
ing difficulties and doubts, Hemingway's heroes grow up, and
step by step their idea of the meaning of life changes and
crystallizes. The struggle of common people for a decent existence, their simple and straightforward attitude towards life and
death, serve as a model for Hemingway's more complex and
contradictory characters. All of them alike are faced with the
problems of fear, violence and death; they solve them in different ways, but the best among them look for support to life,
strength, and courage." The Spanish environment is painted
so glowingly by Hemingway because the people have maintained certain past traditions which are applicable to the present crisis of the "lost generation." It is curious to note that
Spain kept to a policy of neutrality in World War I, and
therefore the Spanish setting has little association with the late
bloody struggle for Jake and his companions. Romero, the
bullfighter, with a quite late entrance into the novel—not until
two-thirds of the way through the text does one see the young
matador—completely entrances the American. Here is a Spaniard, the people whom Jake and/or Hemingway extols, for
whom life is a constant physical ritual with death.

JAKE AS AN "AFICIONADO":   In the first part of Book
Two, Jake was introduced as an *aficionado* by Montoya and his
knowledge about the arrival of the bulls helped his comrades
to enjoy the spectacle even more. In these chapters, however,
Jake comes front and center as an authority more versed in the
national sport than most Spaniards. Hemingway's descriptions
of the actual bullfight scenes are recognized by pro and con
critics, and these scenes exist in abundance as the outstanding
narrative feature of *The Sun Also Rises*. In fact, they are admired as some of the most sparkling pages he wrote; even in
Spain, Hemingway won applause for his reportorial and yet
emotional expressions of the bullfight; he also popularized
throughout the world the rather unknown annual *fiesta* of Pamplona. He warms up to his subject gradually and toys with the

reader in sparse and dry accounts of the bullfights during the first two days in Chapter XV; even his pages in Chapter XVII about the running of the bulls are prosaic.

For Jake, the "moment of truth," when a man is within range of death and nothing in the past matters, erupts in Chapter XVIII, perhaps one of the most beautiful, dramatic, and skillful chapters of Hemingway's writings.

PEDRO ROMERO: Although the bullfighter talks little and takes no part in the party of Jake, he controls the action of these chapters. He is talked about, he is seen; but the matador himself is generally silent, and the "silences" of Hemingway's characters have been commented upon by several critics. For instance, Melvin Blackman writes that "Pedro was exempt from the *mal de siècle* that beset the others, for his fighting with the bulls brought him into a fundamental relationship with life, which involved the pitting of his maleness against that of the bull. It is a life and death struggle that reveals not only the steel of his young manhood but a certain passion with which he met life—an intensity, a seriousness, a dedicated quality. Pedro had a place in the scheme of existence—and a role to fulfill." Romero is uncorrupted by the mood of the "lost generation"; and he has none of the anguish of the others. It is possible that Hemingway is advocating this course of return to a more primitive and natural way of life; certainly Romero is finely etched and held up to perfection by the author.

For that reason, some critics have concluded that Pedro Romero is really the "hero" of *The Sun Also Rises*. Always the bystander and never fully the participant, Jake recedes in importance not because of the lack of a central role in the novel, which he certainly has in these chapters, but because of his inability to provide a positive note to the proceedings. In short, the "moral center" of the book has been awarded at times to Pedro Romero. Backman agrees with this analysis and supports the argument in these words: "With the instinctive sureness of a primitive who need never question his reason for living, he pursued his natural course. And it was this which even Brett came to recognize. There was an absolute center to him. He did not have to drink, he did not have to keep running away. His inner core was brought into a vital active relationship with life. As Jake commented, it is only a bullfighter who lives life to the hilt, bringing to his work all his courage, intelligence, discipline, and art."

Nevertheless, the true test of Pedro Romero's manhood does not come in the bullfight arena but in his encounter with Robert Cohn. It is true that Hemingway has demonstrated again his technical skill in the handling of the affair: he has devoted some of his most beautiful pages to the description of the bullfight, and a great deal of suspense is built up about the fate of the matador.

Pedro Romero has formed for himself a code, admittedly a code based upon primitive instincts and a simple way of life but a code which is effective and noble. Here, then, is Hemingway's answer for the moral dilemma of the "lost generation": an appreciation and adaptation of the untamed qualities of the elementary man. Robert Cohn and Jake Barnes stand at the extreme edges of this center: Cohn employs physical strength without respect for life or death in a warped version of manliness; and Jake agonizes in his frustration and loneliness.

MIKE CAMPBELL AND BILL GORTON: Both friends are in evidence throughout the chapters of this part but they conversely have little to contribute to Hemingway's themes and ideas. There is absolutely no hope for Mike not only in the world of the twenties but even in the escapist environment of the "lost generation." If anything, he is more "lost" than any other participant in this "lost generation."

ROBERT COHN: Hemingway reserves his sharpest verbal

attacks against Robert Cohn, and therefore he may have been criticizing false literary ideals as Stewart Sanderson suggests: "Hemingway's portrayal of the lineaments of Cohn's character reflects one of his basic tenets. Literature must not be confused with life; nor real feelings with what one is expected to feel or think. Part of Cohn's touble is that he has got too many of his ideas out of books . . . and this is no guide for an imperfect American Jew embarking on a temporary *liaison* with a dipsomaniac in a hotel in San Sebastian. Hemingway has expressed his distrust of the fake literary response on many occasions; and in the fictional character of Robert Cohn he presents a study of dishonest and fake emotional behaviour."

MINOR CHARACTERS: The minor characters add to the atmosphere of gaiety, excitement, and color which the escapist *fiesta* of Pamplona signifies. Edna is a young American friend of Bill whom he meets accidentally in the town; she remains in the background and joins with the others in the celebrations. There seems to be no readily apparent reason for her inclusion in the novel, so that Edna may be only another extraneous character so common in Hemingway's novels. The German *maitre d'hôtel* supplies the sole jarring note among the minor characters, and Hemingway goes to the trouble of imitating his bad pronunciation to emphasize his obnoxious personality. Hemingway achieves through his masterly use of dialogue what more traditional novelists secure through description.

The Spaniards are divided into two categories: the joyful and exuberant witnesses who are there to enjoy and not to face death. They are probably Hemingway's idealization of the Spanish people, and they certainly fit the stereotyped pattern of "Sunny Spain." Penniless but hospitable, these inhabitants of Pamplona and the visitors also resemble the Spanish previously encountered in the other chapters of Book Two. They add to Hemingway's milieu of the *fiesta*. However, the natives who are associated with Romero and the bullfights are of a dif-

ferent breed; in fact, they oppose the others almost diametric-
ally in temperament and bearing. This sober bearing is the reflection of their knowledge of the seriousness of the festivities
and the proximity of death. The best example of the Spaniards
in the text and of this particular group is Montoya.

COMMENT

DEATH: Death in various forms pervades these chapters of
the second book. For example, it appears in a happy moment,
the running of the bulls, and comes unexpectedly, suddenly,
and cruelly. A character who has no part in the action is killed:
Vicente Girones, a twenty-eight year old peasant visiting the
fiesta. This seemingly obscure fact has bearing on the novel and
the protagonists as Earl Rovit indicates: "For Girones is a
symbol of the fatal and unchangeable stakes that are involved
in the game that all the characters are playing. He leaves his
wife and two children to run with the bulls, but he must pay
with his life for his 'fun.' Bill and the others have become
practised in ignoring the prices they will have to pay for the
'fun' also. The consequence of their variety of self-deceit is a
constant death-in-life because they have chosen to accept the
rule of nothingness, becoming servitors to its reign in the
frenzy of their acceptance. Girones' death is the physical fact
of their living deaths, and their inability to respond to it establishes clearly to what extent they have died." Thus, death
enters as a central motif on the physical level first of all: it
may be anticipated or unanticipated. The latter situation is
portrayed by the goring of Girones.

SYMBOLISM: First, one must recall the favorite symbol of
the mountains and the plains, emphasized so much by Carlos
Baker, Hemingway's official biographer. A descent from high
places to lower geographical sites indicates that a change for
the worse in the hero's fortunes will ensue. Thus, the return

from Burguete to Pamplona foreshadows unpleasant complications; this alteration is confirmed in the tensions and frictions among Brett's lovers. In this second part of Book Two (and again it should be kept in mind that the division is quite arbitrary because Hemingway includes two-thirds of *The Sun Also Rises* within the confines of this second book) the weather enters to add to the geographical symbolism. For example, the sun indicates that life is pleasant and that the party is having a good time; the bullfights take place obviously in the sunshine, and these events focus the attention of the protagonists. However, the implications of trouble come early: at the end of Chapter XIV, Jake wakes up in the morning to discover that it "had rained" during the night and then observes that the "plateau" seems "fresh and cool."

Of course, the great triumph of Pedro Romero happens in the bright sunlight because he is the victor of this part of Book Two. Another interesting symbol, noted by Carlos Baker and others, is the fear which the main characters will have of the darkness.

FURTHER SYMBOLISM: The darkness is the time when the characters are totally alone: there is no noise or frantic activity to lull their disturbed moods. The "Hemingway Hero" is a man of action and not of contemplation; therefore, he wants the daylight when he can see and do things. Even in broad daylight, the characters do not like to remain alone; they search company to keep them occupied and prevent them from thinking.

The "church" is also a covert but recurring symbol in the progress of these chapters.

Not all critics are in agreement about the significance of the words of the texts as symbols. Malcolm Cowley and E. M. Halliday do not accept fully the emphasis accorded these terms by

Carlos Baker, although the first two critics do stress the artistry previously ignored in Ernest Hemingway's simple style. And indeed, as one reads the text, one should note carefully the vocabulary of Hemingway and try to decide the degree of validity in previous criticism by oneself.

BOOK THREE

(Chapter XIX)

CHARACTER ANALYSES

MINOR CHARACTERS: Only a few, nameless persons enter the action of this very short last chapter, but they offer a passing comment on the change of mood after the vacation period. All the few minor characters sharply contrast with the pleasant peasants of Pamplona. For instance, Hemingway makes some biting comments about France and the French at several places in Chapter XIX. It is curious that in these closing, pathetic pages, the novelist apparently hints that the environment and the natives are no longer able to suffice the restlessness and soul-searching of his "lost generation" types.

COMMENT

STRUCTURE: When one recalls the very long Book Two of *The Sun Also Rises,* the twenty pages of Book Three almost resemble an epilogue. And it could be considered a postscript or a last turn of the screw by the novelist since all the action of the novel has properly occurred by the end of the second book. Strictly speaking, Hemingway could have logically terminated his story without Book Three, and the novel would have had a definite unity and structure. However, the short Chapter XIX gives fuller import to the theme of *The Sun Also Rises* as Philip Young explains: "Then, in an intensely muted coda, a solitary Jake, rehabilitating himself, washes away his hangovers in the ocean. Soon it is all gone, he is returned to Brett as before, and we discover that we have come full circle, like all the rivers, the winds, and the sun, to the place where we began."

THE BOOK'S CYCLE: In other words, a cycle of existence has been completed, and the characters are still trapped by life's anxieties and their own myriad and complex problems. However, this cyclical unity of the novel illustrates acutely the motif of the "lost generation," and Max Herzberg summarizes in this manner: "The fact that nothing really leads anywhere in the novel points to its central theme; the action comes full circle to imitate the sun which as described in Ecclesiastes, also rises only to hasten to the place where it arose." Without the concluding chapter, then, the introductory quotation from the Bible and the title of the book would have been meaningless or at least incomplete. With the last episode, the theme and the implications of the problems of the nineteen twenties acquire forceful meaning.

THE CHIEF PROTAGONISTS: Since Jake and Brett are the principal protagonists of *The Sun Also Rises,* it behooves Hemingway to demonstrate clearly and emphatically how they render valid his concepts of the "Hemingway Code" and the "Hemingway Hero." While they are both hopelessly trapped within their personalities and their environmental situations, their postures at the last moment are not the same. Jake is more mature than Brett but even he has not succeeded in perfecting more than a negative approach to the world which he is reentering. There is no optimistic or at least constructive philosophy to serve as a guide for himself, his friends, and the "lost generation." Thus, Mark Spilka in his affirmation of the concept of the "death of love" as a predominant motif in *The Sun Also Rises* concludes with this intriguing analysis: "In fact, it is the bullfighter who seems to abide in the novel, for surely the bulls are dead like the trout before them, having fulfilled their roles as beloved opponents. But Romero is very much alive as the novel ends.

When he leaves the hotel in Madrid, he 'pays the bill' for his affair with Brett, which means that he has earned all its benefits. He also dominates the final conversation between the lovers, and so dominates the closing section. . . . In this sense, Pedro is the real hero of the parable, the final moral touchstone, the man whose code gives meaning to a world where love and religion are defunct, where the proofs of manhood are difficult and scarce, and where every man must learn to define his own moral conditions and then live up to them."

Nevertheless, the main thrust of Hemingway's purpose is toward the inability of his expatriates to secure a foothold on the vast continent of their age. The effect is certainly depressing as the reader feels that Brett and Jake will wander about Paris and other places searching for and not finding any security. It is even doubtful whether they will enjoy each other's company again, and certainly no grand reunion at Pamplona or some other site will reoccur. In fact, none of Hemingway's novels has a "happy" ending, and *The Sun Also Rises* early foreshadowed this technical procedure of Hemingway.

GENERAL CHARACTER ANALYSES

JAKE BARNES: Since Jake is the narrator of the novel, certain problems arise from this circumstance and his peculiar physical condition as Earl Rovit notes: "The difficulties of interpreting *The Sun Also Rises* in a clear and relatively certain manner stem in the main from two factors: the use of a particularly opaque first-person narrator; and the fact of Jake's wound which has rendered him impotent, while leaving him normally responsive to sexual desire. The first factor results in the bewilderment a reader will have in trying to locate the norms of 'truth' in the novel; that is, since the entire novel is related directly by Jake Barnes, the reader can never be sure how reliable Jake's observations and judgments are. He does not know to what extent he must look at Jake ironically and to what extent sympathetically." Despite the shift in emphasis at times within the novel, Jake remains at the center of the narration; for better or for worse, it is through Jake's eyes that the reader extracts his impressions of the action and the other protagonists. It goes without saying that there are evident autobiographical aspects to Jake's character and his experiences. In fact, *The Sun Also Rises* has been judged as a *roman à clef,* that is to say, a novel in which the characters are identifiable figures from real life.

JAKE'S TRIAL: In the three books of the novel, Jake passes from a stage of anguish and at times self-pity to the acceptance of life on its own terms and the appreciation of nature, companionship, and bravery to his full stature as a man. After these phases, Jake emerges as a "Hemingway Hero": a stoical, cynical, realistic individual who will submerge his feelings within himself and who will await the inevitable reckoning which life presents for the gift of existence.

JAKE'S "CODE":   In some ways, the parting scene at the conclusion of the novel, the farewell of Chapter XIX, bears much resemblance to Book One's ending. In the last chapter, Jake and Brett must bid each other farewell, and the implication is that it will be for the last time, as was hoped for in Book One.

BRETT: Because of her four lovers and the attendant fact that the plot, such as it is, revolves about the ensuing complications, Brett stands out as the most fascinating protagonist of the total group of actors in the novel. To each of her male admirers, Brett is different; she also has a distinct attitude toward them as Carlos Baker observes: "One of the ironies in the portrait of Brett is her ability to appreciate quality in the circle of her admirers."

In her ostentatious flouting of the rules of society and morality, Brett is apparently secure and happy; however, the contrary situation is true. Brett, standing up to be counted in her "moment of truth," nevertheless acquires no additional traits of the code. Without doubt, Brett is a very colorful personality and adds an exotic but compelling portrait to Hemingway's gallery of protagonists.

ROBERT COHN: Hemingway has penned one of the most bitter verbal depictions of a character in his entire literary output in Robert Cohn. He is the complete opposite of the "Hemingway Hero"; he has no understanding or appreciation of the code, and for these reasons he has the signs of a caricature occasionally. Hemingway probably described Cohn as a Jew, not for any overt demonstration of anti-Semitism but to explain part of the young man's problem. Some critics have read into this character a Hemingway attack on the defects of the American character. If this is true, and there seems to be more than a modicum of accuracy in the criticism, then the unfavorable attributes of American youth are: a basic immaturity, reliance upon physical strength, a thin veneer of romanticism, the lack of appreciation for the simple virtues of companionship, good food and drink, and the inability to adjust to the demands of an older civilization. The world of Hemingway is a man's world; Hemingway always sets up on a pedestal the "he-man." Cohn is an example of the "boy-man," the adolescent playing at the role of a mature individual. Without Cohn's presence in the novel, the positive virtues of the code would not have been so fully exemplified; one arrives at a clearer comprehension of Jake Barnes and of Romero's dedication to life and death.

PEDRO ROMERO: The young Spanish matador enters the story late and does not partake of the action in general; in fact, his speeches are extremely limited. However, Romero personifies the ideal which Hemingway found in Spain and in the bullfight. The pages about the *corrida* are among the finest in the history of the literature of this sport because Hemingway not only renders in concise and sparkling prose the exact details of the happenings but also analyzes so brilliantly the psychological frame of reference of the nineteen-year old bullfighter. In many ways, Romero is an idealization of the Spaniard: laconic, proud, honorable, and brave. Romero is untamed by civilization and uncorrupted by the decadence of the modern world so that he is fundamentally a symbol and a stereotype rather than a living person complex to fathom. In addition to the "Spanishness" of the matador, Hemingway has converted this character into a defender of his own literary and personal expression. Romero is the answer to the onslaught of American civilization and youth in the wake of the death of European civilization after World War I. There must be a return to the primitive man, to the simple and direct manner of life he advocates, and to his ability to stand up to death. Pedro Romero is of course the character who has the most dramatic encounter with death, but his "moment of truth" has bearing on the lives of the five friends who are viewing the bullfight. Thus, Mark Spilka concludes that "where Cohn expends and degrades himself for his beloved, Romero pays tribute without self-loss. His manhood is a thing independent of women, and for this reason he holds a special attraction for Jake Barnes." Therefore, the principal contribution of Romero is his exemplification of the code admired by Jake and exploited by him in the "moment of truth" with Brett at the end.

MINOR CHARACTERS: The minor characters can be divided into two categories: those who are extraneous to the action and reflect the European setting, and those who may appear briefly but lend some support to Hemingway's themes and ideas. For example, Edna, the friend of Bill, whom they encounter in Pamplona; and Georgette, the streetwalker, do not contribute any important material to the development of the plot or the comprehension of the protagonists. On the other hand, there are secondary figures who support the novelists's theories. For instance, Count Mippipopolous is the expression of an older man's adjustment to life and to its tragic sense; Wilson-Harris epitomizes the international bond of camaraderie in a "he-man's" world and the worth of friendship; Stewart Sanderson probes the world of Hemingway's characters in this way: "The characterization is excellent; even such minor figures as Zizi the portrait-painter or the anonymous peasants in the bus going up to Burguete come to life in a few swift strokes of the pen. The dialogue is taut and powerful, achieving much of its effect by what is left unsaid but ominously implied and understood. We find, too, Hemingway's gift for recreating in English the flavour of foreign idioms in the speech of the French and Spanish characters." The speech of the characters, major and minor, must be judged in any character analyses since Hemingway relies so heavily on dialogue rather than description for his literary and psychological effects. In fact, one of the great contributions of Hemingway to the novel is the importance accorded to dialogue or what has been dubbed "the art of the unsaid." Sanderson concludes with his essay on the weight of the dialogue in Hemingway's characterization: "He nods only occasionally with an American 'gotten' or 'Are we going down and see those bulls unloaded?' in the mouths of Brett and Mike. Time has taken its toll of some of the slang, while the boisterous schoolboy ragging of Bill and Jake reads a little crudely today."

QUESTIONS AND ANSWERS

1. How does Hemingway sketch the life of the expatriates and at the same time trace the love theme of Jake and Brett?

ANSWER: The group of expatriates in Paris enjoys a series of parties and frivolous activities which nevertheless reveals their basic disorientation and insecurity. The round of party-going demonstrates the fast pace of life of the self-exiles. In the same way, the surface gaiety of the expatriates masks tensions within the group.

The various scenes in Paris between Brett and Jake have a tragic note which contrasts with the apparent joyful pleasures of the others. Thus, there is a comic and a tragic element in the various descriptions of the characters before the action at Pamplona.

2. According to Carlos Baker, Hemingway stated that *The Sun Also Rises* is not a "hollow or bitter satire," but a tragedy. Discuss this interpretation of the novel.

ANSWER: From this point of view, the novel should not be looked upon as a commentary on the "lost generation" or the problem of the expatriates during the nineteen twenties. On the contrary, the novel should be regarded on more personal and individualistic terms, that is to say, it should be judged as the plight of humans caught in a trap of circumstances not entirely of their own making. They are the victims of the war and of a social and political upheaval. In addition to this handicap, they are unable to demonstrate strong personalities which could surmount the influence of the war. In short, they are not persons of strong wills; they do not assert their birthright of life against circumstance. Thus, these characters are tragic because they are unable to prove themselves stronger than the surrounding elements and the past. Even Pedro Romero is tragic because he knows the meaning of death and the risk he faces each time in the bullring. There are no "happy" persons in the novel and of more consequence there is no "happy" ending. The story ends sadly with the defeat of the protagonists, which is a form of death.

3. How does Hemingway employ the ritual of the bullfight in this novel?

ANSWER: The bullfight may be considered as the primitive example and the evident demonstration of the "moment of truth" which Jake already knows comes in the form of "a bill" to be paid. Jake finds in Pedro Romero, unspoiled by modern life and the European collapse, the traits which can be used by his "lost generation." On the first level of interpretation, the bullfight is a direct and physical contest of man against animal or brute force. Man must use all his courage and skill to survive and triumph; he can do so only if he is passive, realistic, and stoical. Some critics have read into the bullfight the struggle between Cohn and Romero; the former is strength without rhyme or reason, and the latter can employ outside the bullfight the same procedures as at the arena. Likewise, the bullfight has been likened to the row between Cohn and Jake with Mike as the *picador* who baits the bull to attack. The main lesson of the bullfight is the application to the perplexing quandry of Jake as to the code he must evolve. Finally, the bullfight shows Hemingway's admiration for Spain and its customs as well as his extraordinary knowledge of the ritual.

4. How does Hemingway utilize vocabulary and syntax to achieve the "Hemingway style"?

ANSWER: In the first place, Hemingway makes use of very simple words, particularly in the dialogue. Even in the descriptive passages, such as the landscape of Spain and the bullfight scenes, the words are still not erudite or literary. For example, Harry Levin calls attention to the fact that Hemingway emphasizes nouns rather than adjectives. The author also repeats certain key words, such as "nice" and "good." Although these are common words and not particularly forceful, the repetition of the terms becomes associated with a character and denotes his personality and his reactions. By using Jake Barnes as the narrator, Hemingway starts many of his sentences abruptly and directly with "I." Showing his long training as a journalist, Hemingway uses short, staccato-like sentences rather than compound and complex sentences. A usual procedure is to use the subject-verb-object combination and to connect the discourse with the word "and." While the effect is easy to read and grasp, the reader feels that he is on very intimate terms with the teller of the story. Another device is to allow the conversation to flow rapidly without indications of any change of speaker; the sentences are shorter than usual when Hemingway is using dialogue. Thus, the conversations are lively, dynamic, and accurate. However, he has been criticized for avoiding colorful and technical words, particularly adjectives, which would contribute depth and variety to his style. In short, Hemingway admittedly avoids the complex in favor of the obvious.

5. What is the significance of the title of the novel, *The Sun Also Rises?*

ANSWER: The quotation from the Old Testament is a cry of pessimism; life moves in cycles, and man is caught within these forces. The constant activity of the earth is really repetitious, and nothing man can do will break the movement of these outside forces. In the novel, there has been little plot and little action; and the characters have not made any progress. Jake and Brett are at exactly the same place they were at the beginning, and the other characters go back to their previous activities or continue their boredom. Time is inexorable, and man's residence on earth is brief. Progress is not a necessary characteristic of life and yet there is no stability or security. For example, the fishing trip of Jake and Bill to Burguete and the poignant farewell of Wilson-Harris to the two were moments which the protagonists would have liked to eternalize. Man can only endeavor to enrich himself by these brief moments of solitude in nature; however, he must pay the "bill" as time and nature's course go on their ways. All the members of the group would prefer that the *fiesta* at Pamplona never terminate and nevertheless they are cognizant that the seven days will be over. There is a constant fleeting of time, no hope of change, and the effort to hold on to happy moments. For example, Brett and Jake would strive if possible to stay together as they are at odd moments of the novel. The search for enlightenment about the meaning of existence is pursued in the midst of this meaningless flux and sameness of time.

6. Malcolm Cowley speaks of the need for rituals, superstitions, symbols, and legends with which Hemingway surrounds his characters. Comment on this theory:

ANSWER: These devices betray the fear and insecurity in which man lives; man surrounds his existence with these rituals to protect himself. The excessive drinking of the entire group of friends is symptomatic of their dread of cold reality; they prefer an alcoholic haze in which to escape from their anxieties. However, all the various mannerisms of the characters in the novel are based on the world-as-it-is; they are true to each other and do not conceal their use of these supports. Even the language is ritualized by the use of certain words repeated often. Good eating and drinking, common items in themselves, are dwelt on lovingly by the author as part of the needed ritual of his actors.

7. Discuss the relationship between the "Hemingway Hero" and the "Hemingway Code."

ANSWER: The "Hemingway Code" is an undefined set of rules by which the characters act out their lives and their relationships with the world and with one another. Directness, honesty, stoicism, and the truth above all, are characteristics of Hemingway's creed of manliness. The "Hemingway Hero" strives to perfect himself according to these principles with varying degrees of success. Usually, the hero has an encounter with an important event which brings the code to bear for the rest of his life. Romero, Jake, and Brett in that order are the epitomes of the code. Only Romero succeeds in dominating the outside world; Brett and Jake still do not make positive overtures toward the contemporary scene. However, they control their inner world as does Romero; the latter reconciles both the concept of the "Hemingway Hero" and the "Hemingway Code."

8. Discuss Hemingway's interest in violence as a theme in *The Sun Also Rises*.

ANSWER: According to Hemingway, man is surrounded by violence, and he must seek to fathom the meaning in this basic aspect of life. Violence is not necessarily pictured for its own sake; for instance, the fight between Romero and Cohn is only related from the angle of a third person. The fight between Jake and Cohn, and then Mike, is sketched in the briefest of words. There is little lesson in the latter episodes unlike the conflict in the bullfight arena. Hemingway has been accused of writing with enthusiasm and enjoyment of violent scenes, but this criticism is not borne out by the evidence of this particular novel. There are no reminiscences of the violent action that Jake and Mike have seen during the war, and Hemingway omitted any details of that war which Cohn wanted to hear from Mike. In short, violence is not brought out abundantly in the novel; however, it does have a definite place in the structural and thematic unity of the novel.

9. Hemingway worked carefully in the composition of his novels and planned thoughtfully the structure as he wrote. Discuss the structural arrangement of *The Sun Also Rises*.

ANSWER: This novel is deceptively simple on the surface and with an apparently unplanned or at least non-serious air. For example, the introductory chapters about Jake's and Cohn's friendship, Jake's love for Brett, and the proposed jaunt to Pamplona seem no more than indications of the Bohemian life led by the expatriates. Another reason for this false impression of the novel is the uneven length of the three parts: the second book comprises most of the novel, and the third book is only a chapter of twenty pages. However, all the strands which the novelist has woven come into their own when Cohn steps to the center of the stage in Pamplona. Then, the purpose of the apparent digressions of the first book is made clear; and now the action, always muted and never the prime attribute of the novel, can proceed with the conflicts among the characters. There is a delicate balance between relaxed and tense moods, peaceful and tumultuous atmospheres, stability and action, in the combination of the Burguete fishing trip and the *fiesta* in Pamplona within the same Book Two. The outbreak of strife among the friends is simultaneous with the crescendo of the bullfight. Finally, the last chapter is so brief because it is like an epilogue bringing Jake and Brett back where they were at the beginning of the story. Like a play, the novel builds up to the climax, maximum dramatic conflict is achieved, and then the solution must be resolved very rapidly for a stunning effect.

CRITICAL COMMENTARY

The standard edition of *The Sun Also Rises* is published by Charles Scribner's Sons, New York, and the first edition was published by that company in 1926. However, the English edition appeared under the title of *Fiesta*. Although the novel received favorable reviews, its popularity did not increase until after the publication of *A Farewell To Arms* in 1929. The critics praised Hemingway for his stylistic breakthrough in the field of the novel whereas the broad reading public was interested in the way Hemingway depicted the "lost generation." In later years, around 1952, critical attention was devoted to the technical and symbolic as well as structural characteristics of the novel.

THE NOVEL AS A STYLISTIC ACHIEVEMENT: All the critics who wrote about *The Sun Also Rises* after its first appearance in 1926 admitted Hemingway's positive contribution to the novel in his reportorial, factual and yet detailed syntax and in the economy of prose with which he expressed his ideas and themes. These were the two facets of his art which impressed the critics; however, there were no stylistic probings of the novel as occurred later. The sparseness and the directness were new characteristics of the American novel. However, the critics also took to task Hemingway for a certain shallowness in his characters, and Harry Levin writes that "the effectiveness of Hemingway's method depends largely upon his keen ear for speech. His conversations are vivid, often dramatic, although he comes to depend too heavily upon them and to scant the other obligations of the novelist. Many of his wisecracks are quotable out of context, but as Gertrude Stein warned him: 'Remarks are not literature.' He can get his story told, and still be as conversational as he pleases, by telling it in the first person." Nevertheless, Hemingway had caught the spirit of an age which welcomed this reaction to the purple prose of the nineteenth century and the wearisome slogans used to stir the masses during World War I. In short, Hemingway brought conversation into the novel in full force; instead of a technical device, conversation or dialogue became the center of plot development and character analysis. For one thing, Hemingway asserted that prose was not the inside ornamentation of the edifice but the very architecture so involved; he said that as a consequence the Baroque or the highly decorative was past.

THE NOVEL AS A CONTEMPORARY PORTRAIT: When the general public returned to the earlier novel after the immediate success of *A Farewell To Arms,* they saw a literary reproduction of the nineteen twenties; in other words, they received visible confirmation of the existence and anxieties of the "lost generation." Philip Young grasps this reason for the novel's reception: "This is motion which goes no place. Constant activity has brought us along with such pleasant, gentle insistence that not until the end do we realize that we have not been taken in, exactly, but taken nowhere; and that, finally, is the point. This is structure as meaning, organization as content. And, as the enormous effect the book had on its generation proved, such a meaning or content was important to 1926. The book touched with delicate accuracy on something big, on things other people were feeling, but too dimly for articulation. Hemingway had deeply felt and understood what was in the wind. Like Brett, who was the kind of woman who sets styles, the book itself was profoundly creative, and had the kind of power that is prototypal." As the legend of Hemingway grew during the nineteen thirties and the nineteen forties, particularly as a result of his exploits during the Spanish Civil War of 1936-39 and World War II, interest in the clearly autobiographical aspects grew. Also, critics tried to decipher the identity of the other protagonists, such as Robert Cohn.

UNFAVORABLE REACTIONS: Not all critics handled Hemingway so gently, and he was taken to task with great severity for his limited range of ideas and characters. For example, already in 1934, the British writer Wyndham Lewis boldly entitled one of his critiques, *The Dumb Ox: A Study of Ernest Hemingway;* and vituperously described Hemingway's "he-man" as follows: "a dull-witted, bovine, monosyllabic simpleton . . . the voice of the 'folk,' of the masses . . . the cannon fodder, the cattle outside the slaughterhouse, serenely chewing the cud — of those to whom things are done, in contrast to those who have executive will and intelligence." As the immediacy of the period of the "lost generation" faded into history, and the world went from the crisis of the Great Depression of the early nineteen thirties to the rise of Fascism and Nazism, the individual problems of the expatriates took on a romantic glow. There were critics who said that Hemingway had no moral, ethical, or social principles to expound and that his characters were only interested in four things: hunting, fishing, bullfighting, and war. For instance, Aldous Huxley and D. S. Savage bitterly attacked Hemingway, and the latter called Hemingway's work "the proletarianization of literature: the adaptation of the technical artistic conscience to the sub-average human consciousness." Ironically, the phraseology of this critic is exactly the type of language which Hemingway criticized and sought to avoid.

MORE UNFAVORABLE CRITICISM: Sean O'Faolain writes of Hemingway in *The Vanishing Hero* that "his Hero is always as near as makes no matter to being brainless, has no past, no traditions, and no memories." Edmund Wilson and Leslie Fiedler wrote disparagingly of the female person in Hemingway's writings. Leon Edel called the Hemingway creations an example of "superficial action almost wholly without reflection." In other words, as numerous imitators of the Hemingway style, hero, and code appeared, critics searched for character analysis, social context, and positive ideals. The original style and the theme of the "lost generation" were put aside and consequently Hemingway was tried and found wanting. Nevertheless, the novel was immensely popular, and the human appeal it had was not given sufficient attention by critical comment. For instance, Stewart Sanderson ably sums up the novel's perennial lure: "The staying-power of the novel lies partly in the firm moral tone that sustains it, partly in the sheer virtuosity of the writing. It is worth-while remarking that the English edition was published under the title *Fiesta:* the reader is swept along in a mood of tense excitement and elation. The brilliance of the descriptive passages; the finely-cut, many-faceted dialogue from which penetrating rays reflect upon and illuminate the characters and action; the dramatic presentation, all combine to give it a compelling vitality. There is a freshness on the polished surface which time has not dulled, and the total impact of the book is so attractive that we are sometimes in danger of forgetting the essential corruption of the damned and the condemned." After World War II, a new wave of enthusiasm for the novel came about, and a film version was produced in Hollywood. Perhaps because of the traumatic experiences of the generation who had just lived through the global conflict, the "lost generation" of Hemingway's novel received new popular acclaim and sales. Perhaps because the generation of the late nineteen forties and the nineteen fifties could see themselves in the expatriates of the nineteen twenties, Hemingway's message was reevaluated, and *The Sun Also Rises* was often indicated as enjoying more attention from the reading public than *A Farewell To Arms,* which ironically had been Hemingway's mainstay in the financial sweepstakes.

THE NOVEL AS A WORK OF ART: About 1952, although it is obviously impossible to pinpoint an exact date, a "new look" was taken by the critics at all of Hemingway's work in the wake of increased popular interest in *The Sun Also Rises* and other works. However, this particular novel had started to gain in attention and is surely ranked as one of the three best of Hemingway's novels. Since 1950, three collections of essays on Hemingway have appeared by McCaffery, Baker, and Weeks. In 1952, Carlos Baker, who became Hemingway's official biographer, began to publish his contributions to Hemingway criticism. Critics also began to doubt that Hemingway's writings were as simple as they were said to be; for instance, Philip Young in 1952 published a psychobiographical study of Hemingway in which he asserted that the characters, particularly the "Hemingway Hero" in the works, are really complex individuals instead of primitive types. According to Young, the heroes are clothed in rituals, symbols, and legends. Malcolm Cowley also emphasized that the characters are not so extrovert as is supposed; the critic must view their inner motivations and attitudes. Baker in his growing canon of Hemingway critiques stressed the major role of symbolism in the writings. The old canard that Hemingway was essentially "anti-intellectual" was dispelled by interviews with him which revealed his wide reading and his careful craftsmanship. Of course, the award of the Nobel Prize for Literature in 1954 to Hemingway stimulated researchers; and the annual bibliographies prove that in the last ten years more and more articles and books have been done on Hemingway.

If there is any noticeable trend in this research, it is toward the explanation not so much of the characters and the themes but the artistic vision of Hemingway. For example, interest in the structural arrangement of the novels has been undertaken. As a result of this revival of the past ten years or so in Hemingway, the worth of *The Sun Also Rises* has been more recognized, and Robert Weeks concludes that "These evaluations are but another way of saying that Hemingway's art does lack a broad base. He has won his reputation as an artist of the first rank by operating within limits that would have stifled a lesser writer. But within and because of these limits, he has in his best work uttered a lyric cry that — although it may not resemble the full orchestra of Tolstoy or the organ tones of Melville — is nonetheless a moving and finely wrought response to our times." And Philip Young, one of the outstanding new critics on Hemingway, places *The Sun Also Rises* as "one of the two best novels he has written."

BIBLIOGRAPHY

Adams, Richard P., "Sunrise out of the Waste Land." *Tulane Studies in English,* IX (1959), 119-131. (Hemingway influenced by Eliot's poem in *The Sun Also Rises.*)

Atkins, John A., *The Art of Ernest Hemingway,* London, 1952. (A critical evaluation of Hemingway from the point of view of style and and technique generally.)

Baker, Carlos, *Hemingway: The Writer as Artist,* 3rd ed., Princeton, 1964. (An important study with much factual information by Hemingway's official biographer.)

Baker, Carlos, ed., *Hemingway and his Critics,* New York, 1961. (A collection of international scope of reprinted articles.)

Baker, Carlos, ed., *Ernest Hemingway: Critiques of Four Major Novels,* New York, 1962. (Interesting for comparisons and contrasts of Hemingway's works.)

Canby, Henry Seidel, Introduction, *The Sun Also Rises,* Modern Library Edition, New York, 1930.

Cargill, Oscar, *Intellectual America: Ideas on the March,* New York, 1948. (A very subjective but stimulating critique of Hemingway.)

Cohen, Joseph, "Wouk's *Morningstar* and Hemingway's *Sun,*" *South Atlantic Quarterly,* LVIII (1959), 213-24.

Fenton, Charles A., *The Apprenticeship of Ernest Hemingway,* New York, 1954. (A scholarly investigation and documented biography of Hemingway's early years until 1925.)

Fiedler, Leslie A., *Love and Death in the American Novel,* Cleveland, 1962. (A Freudian interpretation of the symbolism and images of Hemingway's novels.)

Halliday, E. M., "Hemingway's Hero," *University of Chicago Magazine,* XLV (1953), 10-14.

Halliday, E. M., "Hemingway's Narrative Perspective," *Sewanee Review,* LX (1952), 202-18.

Lewis, Wyndham, *Men Without Art,* London, 1934, pp. 17-40. (An unfavorable attitude toward Hemingway and his writings.)

Isabelle, Julanne, *Hemingway's Religious Experience,* New York, 1964. (Tries to see a deep religious anguish in Hemingway.)

Killinger, John, *Hemingway and the Dead Gods: A Study in Existentialism,* Lexington, 1961.

Loeb, Harold. "The Young Writer in Paris and Pamplona." *Saturday Review,* XLIV (29 July 1961), 25-26.

McCaffery, John K. M., ed., *Ernest Hemingway: The Man and His Work,* Cleveland, 1950. (A pioneer effort at compiling essays about Hemingway.)

Moore, Geoffrey. *"The Sun Also Rises:* Notes Toward an Extreme Fiction." *Review of English Literature* (Leeds, England), IV, iv, 31-46.

Nishiyama, Tamotsu. "Hemingway's Post-War Generation Reconsidered." *North Dakota Quarterly,* XXVIII (1960), 129-133.

Rovit, Earl, *Ernest Hemingway,* New York, 1963. (A critical examination of the themes and artistic principles of Hemingway.)

Sanderson, Stewart, *Ernest Hemingway,* New York, 1961. (A brief but penetrating insight into Hemingway's work.)

Scott, Arthur L., "In Defense of Robert Cohn," *College English,* XVIII (1957), 309-14.

Stephens, Robert O. "Hemingway's Don Quixote in Pamplona." *College English,* XXIII (1962), 216-18. (An interpretation of Cohn.)

Warren, Robert Penn. "Hemingway," *Kenyon Review, IV* (Winter, 1947), 1-28. (An investigation into the meanings of the Hemingway code.)

Weeks, Robert P., ed., *Hemingway: A Collection of Critical*

Essays, Englewood Cliffs, N. J., 1962 (An important series of previously published critiques on Hemingway and his work.)

Young, Philip, *Ernest Hemingway,* New York, 1952. (A stimulating psychobiographical analysis of Hemingway's work.)

NOTES

NOTES

MONARCH® NOTES AND STUDY GUIDES

ARE AVAILABLE AT RETAIL STORES EVERYWHERE

In the event your local bookseller cannot provide you with other Monarch titles you want —

ORDER ON THE FORM BELOW:

Complete order form appears on inside front & back covers for your convenience.

Simply send retail price, local sales tax, if any, plus 35¢ per book to cover mailing and handling.

TITLE #	AUTHOR & TITLE (exactly as shown on title listing)	PRICE
PLUS ADDITIONAL 35¢ PER BOOK FOR POSTAGE		
	GRAND TOTAL	$

MONARCH® PRESS, a Simon & Schuster Division of Gulf & Western Corporation
Mail Service Department, 1230 Avenue of the Americas, New York, N.Y. 10020

I enclose $ .... to cover retail price, local sales tax, plus mailing and handling.

Name _____
(Please print)
Address _____

City _____ State _____ Zip _____

Please send check or money order. We cannot be responsible for cash.